IMAGES
of America

TURTLE BACK ZOO

IMAGES
of America

TURTLE BACK ZOO

Brint Spencer and Caitlin A. Sharp

ARCADIA
PUBLISHING

Published by Arcadia Publishing
Charleston, South Carolina

Library of Congress Control Number: 2013937874

For all general information, please contact Arcadia Publishing:
Telephone 843-853-2070
Fax 843-853-0044
E-mail sales@arcadiapublishing.com
For customer service and orders:
Toll-Free 1-888-313-2665

Visit us on the Internet at www.arcadiapublishing.com

To Walt and Peg Spencer, who always encouraged my interest in animals, accepted my fascination with snakes, developed my interest in history and supported me throughout my career. —Brint

To two people who met at a zoo, fell in love, and went on to raise an animal-loving, tree-hugging, people-person just like them . . . I love you, Mom & Dad. —Caitlin

CONTENTS

ACKNOWLEDGMENTS

Histories of the Turtle Back Zoo have been compiled for various reasons, but no history had ever been produced for people to reminisce or learn from. What better occasion to compile information and images of the zoo than on its 50th anniversary in 2013?

Special thanks to the many people who make up the County of Essex, particularly county executive Joseph N. DiVincenzo Jr. and the Essex County Board of Chosen Freeholders, and Dan Salvante, director of parks and recreation, whose support of the zoo shows no limits.

Sifting through historical documents and pictures can be an arduous task, but it was made lighter with access to the Essex County Parks Historic Documents Library. The help of parks archivist Kathy Kauhl and research and archival assistant Rakhi Upadhyay is appreciated.

The support of the Zoological Society of New Jersey and executive director Adam Kerins helped to bring this project to fruition. Zoological society intern Jeniffer Saavedra was extremely helpful when it came to organizing historical items and photographs collected by the zoo over the years.

The staff at a facility is always a vital resource for historical data. This book would not have been completed without the memorabilia, photographs, and memories of past and current Turtle Back Zoo staff, especially former zoo director Jeremy Goodman, former longtime employee Sue Mitschke, former zoo curator Richard Freitag, and current zoo supervisor Gina Zullo.

Special thanks go to Vince and Elaine Sharp. Your memories litter the pages of this book. Thank you for helping make this a story not just of a zoo and its animal collection, but of the people that worked there and visited over the years.

Unless otherwise noted, photographs in this book are courtesy of the facility archives of the Essex County Turtle Back Zoo.

INTRODUCTION

On March 5, 1895, the first county park system in the United States was established when Gov. George Werts of New Jersey signed legislation creating the Essex County Park Commission. Frederick Law Olmsted, the nation's foremost landscape architect, described the South Mountain Reservation as some of the most beautiful terrain he had seen. In 1898, the Olmsted Brothers firm designed all the parks and reservations of the Essex County Park System and produced one of the nation's finest park systems.

In 1962, the Essex County Park Commission awarded a contract to build a zoo on a 15.5-acre section of the county's South Mountain Reservation. The $400,000 facility was the culmination of seven years of planning and one year of construction. Funds used were derived from the sale of county lands to the state for highway purposes. Tjark Reiss of New York was hired to design the zoo. He created exhibits based on Hans Christian Anderson's nursery rhymes and other children's stories. Exhibits included the Old Lady in the Shoe, Mother Goose, and Humpty Dumpty. There was a castle occupied by prairie dogs, a Swiss cheese wedge with a South American capybara, and a European hedgehog. The entrance and administration buildings resembled a country village from those stories. The zoo also featured a New England farm, complete with barn and corral. Area farmers leased young animals in the spring and took them back at the end of the season. A scaled-down winter staff was needed to care for animals, such as the buffalo, yak, elk, and exotic sheep, that wintered at Turtle Back Zoo. An animal ring allowed children to handle and pet small animals like rabbits, kittens, and guinea pigs. Zooettes, paid employees attired in blue skirts and red-and-white checkered shirts, were available to supervise the animal handling. A miniature antique train, the Iron Horse, took visitors on a mile-long ride through the zoo's surrounding woodlands.

The zoo took its name from a rock formation located on the mountainside just east of the zoo. The Lenape Indians called this formation Turtle Back Rock. The pattern on the rocks, created by large basaltic crystals, gives the impression of the back of an enormous tortoise.

Turtle Back Zoo officially opened at 3:00 p.m. on June 2, 1963. The zoo opened to the public on June 3, 1963, with a collection of 140 animals of 40 species. Later that year, a $5,000 gift was made to be used for a Star of the Week exhibit, which would feature different animals each week. Part of the gift was used for flight cages located on the periphery of the children's area, which housed colorful foreign and domestic birds. In June 1965, Richard Ryan, a well-known ornithologist from the Bronx Zoo, was hired as the director. He began to move the zoo's development beyond the seasonal children's zoo concept. The next year, a 13,000-gallon exhibit of three sea lions was added. This rapidly became a very popular attraction.

Although the zoo remained closed for the winter, educational programs continued during the cold months. Staff members brought animals to different groups and institutions, discussing nature, species, habits, and habitats. A variety of animals were brought to schools and to the pediatric section of local hospitals. A specially equipped Zoomobile transported the animals and their keepers. Overall, 100 programs were presented annually. By the 1970s, Turtle Back Zoo became a year-round recreational and educational facility with approximately 450 animals of 120 species. The zoo also became a botanical center. To aid in erosion control, and for aesthetic reasons, 1,500 trees and shrubs were planted. Many of the trees and shrubs were labeled with their names and the purposes for which they were used.

In 1971, the Tortoisry was built. This building was dedicated to the housing, exhibiting, and breeding of turtles from around the world. Many endangered species have been successfully bred, and the resulting offspring and breeding research were shared with other zoos and conservation organizations. A new Education Center was built and in use by 1974. It included a large room for live animal presentations, animal nursery, classrooms, and a first-aid office. With its four staff members, the building and its programming rivaled any zoo education in the country. In 1975, the zoo created a zoological society for promotion and to provide funding and support through memberships and other fundraising activities.

In May 1979, the park commission was replaced by the Essex County Department of Parks, Recreation and Cultural Affairs, which took over the responsibility for park development, maintenance, and programs. The department also took on the artistic, cultural, and historic preservation responsibilities of the former Cultural and Heritage Commission.

After years of insufficient funding, the zoo fell into disrepair. The county considered closing it in the mid-1990s. After public outcry, the decision was made to keep the zoo open, and improvements were made to the facilities. The Essex County Board of Chosen Freeholders began a major infrastructure upgrade, led by Joseph N. DiVincenzo. Many major drainage issues were addressed at this time, and new animal fencing and pavement was installed.

In 2006, a new master plan was commissioned to ensure the continued growth and stability of the zoo. Also that year, the zoo became accredited by the Association of Zoos and Aquariums for the first time in its history.

Recent additions have included Wild New Jersey, an exhibit educating visitors about New Jersey's native wildlife; an endangered species carousel; Asian and Australian section, with a walk-through aviary; and, in 2013, a sea lion exhibit to celebrate the zoo's 50th anniversary. In addition, the old penguin exhibit was renovated.

One

THE 1960s
WHY A ZOO IN ESSEX COUNTY?

Over the years, educators, civic groups, and individuals expressed the need for a zoo in heavily populated Essex County. As early as 1938, the *Newark Ledger* reported on a submitted proposal by Abraham Schindel, general manager of Hearns-Newark Department Store, for a zoo in the South Mountain Reservation. Schindel had been sponsoring an exhibit of Frank Buck's jungle camp at the store. In a two-week period, over 75,000 people paid a small fee to go through the camp to see the animals. This helped to legitimize the clamor for a zoo in the area.

In time, the Essex County Park Commission directed its staff to prepare a report that would recommend a concept of the type of zoo that might be built within the commission's financial limitations and a specific site for it. The zoo study involved trips to many zoos in the Eastern United States, conferences with zoo directors, and countless staff meetings.

A children-oriented zoo, designed to effectively utilize a 15-acre wooded tract in the northeastern part of South Mountain Reservation, was recommended. Still, the decision to build a zoo was a difficult one. This would commit the commission to an entirely different phase of recreation. Plans would have to envision aesthetic values as well as practical use. Pittsburgh's Highland Park Zoo had recently completed a children's zoo, the planning of which had been done by architect W. Tjark Reiss. A visit to the zoo convinced the staff that he was the right person to design a zoo for Essex County.

As a starting point, every tree of any consequence was plotted, and Reiss planned the zoo so as to preserve them. Trees would play an important part in overall aesthetics, their charm and shade enhancing the creative design. Exhibits would be based on Hans Christian Anderson's nursery rhymes and other children's stories. The zoo would also feature a New England farm, complete with barn, silo, and corral. As architectural plans neared completion, the park commission and its staff began to get "zoo fever." The long-awaited vision of a zoo in Essex County came to life when the Turtle Back Zoo officially opened to the public on June 3, 1963, with a collection of 140 animals of 40 species.

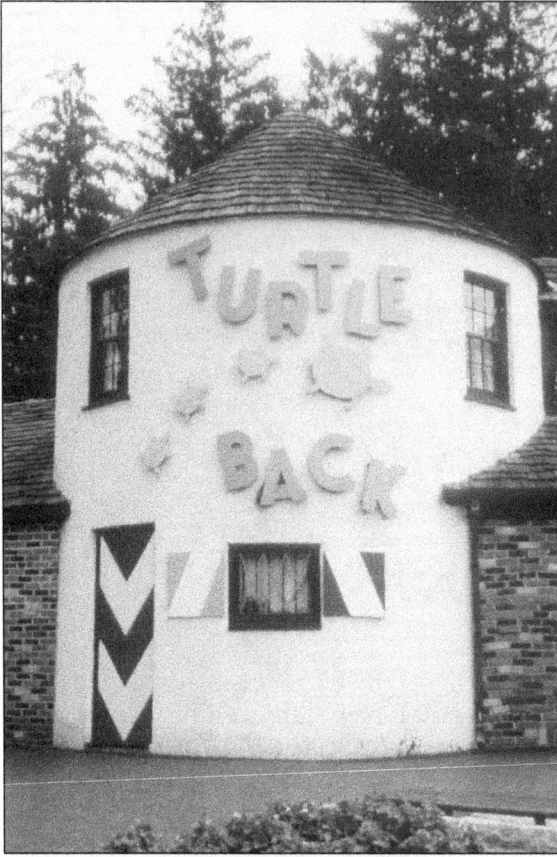

For 50 years, the zoo entrance has been dominated by its iconic twin turrets. Except for cosmetic upkeep, they have remained the same. Alterations have been made, however, to the area inside and around the turrets. The circular interior rooms have changed functions, from a birthday party room to zoo library, then as storage, and finally office space.

When the zoo opened, one of the greatest surprises was the demand for souvenirs. Here is one of the many postcards that could be purchased at the zoo gift shop. A view of the original front entrance shows off the towers and carefully planned, separated entrance and exit gates. Later, the front would be expanded to be more accommodating and safer as well as more attractive, with landscaping and brick walkways.

The zoo took its name from a rock formation located on the mountainside just to the east in the South Mountain Reservation. The pattern on the rocks was created when basalt lava flowed through the Newark rift basin valley and then cooled and fractured into small hexagonal blocks. The large basaltic crystals form the impression of the back of an enormous tortoise. The Lenape Indians named this formation Turtle Back Rock.

For the first two years of the zoo's existence, children were most often found riding on the backs of the 250-pound Aldabra tortoises. Sometimes, other zoo animals would be intrigued enough to try turtle-riding themselves. Although not the fastest ride, this was quite a memorable experience. (Courtesy of Sue Mitschke.)

THE ANIMALS OF

Turtle

ZOO

BACK

TURTLE BACK ZOO
NORTHFIELD AVENUE
(In back of South Mountain Arena)
WEST ORANGE, N. J.
A facility of Essex County Park Commission

This guidebook from the 1960s was the first produced by the Turtle Back Zoo. It was in the form of a walking tour through each area of the zoo. Information for each animal was presented in an "a" section for adults and a simplified "b" section designed to be read to children at the exhibit.

Turtle Back Zoo officially opened at 3:00 p.m. on June 2, 1963, in a ceremony attended by various dignitaries. The zoo opened to the public on June 3, with a collection of 140 animals of 40 species. The hours were 10:00 a.m. to 6:00 p.m. on weekdays and 10:00 a.m. to 8:00 p.m. on weekends and holidays during the summer months. During the first three weeks of operation, there were 67,774 visitors, 10,000 of which came on the first Sunday; 8,000 visitors came to the zoo on June 16, and 9,000 on June 23. The income for the first season was $47,327, and it was expected that admissions and other revenues would allow the zoo to be self-sustaining.

TURTLE BACK ZOO

A FACILITY OF THE

ESSEX COUNTY PARK COMMISSIO

OPENING SPRING 1963

ARCHITECT W. TJARK REISS
CONTRACTORS
GENERAL MAX DRILL, INC. NEWARK, N
ELECTRICAL LIGHTNING ELECTRIC CO. NEWARK, N
PLUMBING ALLAN E. BROWN MAPLEWOOD,
PLUMBING & HEATING CO.

This dedication plaque was located just to the right of the zoo's main gate. The medallion in the lower-right corner features the Turtle Back Zoo logo. The one on the left side lists the various exhibits and activities the visitor could enjoy at the zoo, including the Mayflower, Octopus, Children's Zoo, train, and Eating House.

One could always spot a Zooette, due to their signature red-and-white checkered shirts and navy blue pants or skirts during the summer, as well as their friendly smile. *Zooette*, a term used to describe employees who worked on zoo grounds with the public, grew out of favor in the late 1970s and early 1980s.

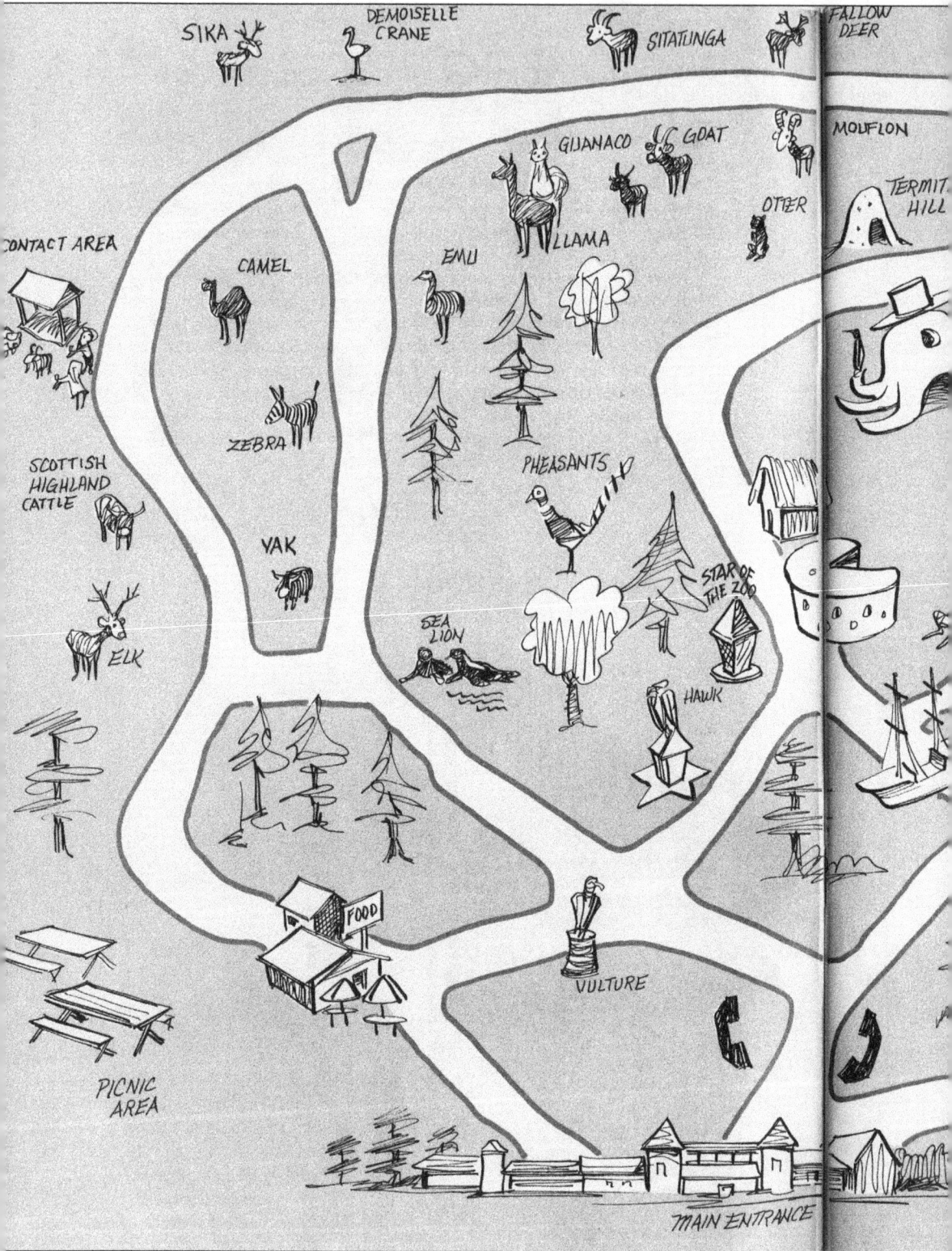

SIKA

DEMOISELLE
CRANE

SITATUNGA

FALLOW
DEER

GUANACO

GOAT

MOUFLON

CONTACT AREA

CAMEL

EMU

LLAMA

OTTER

TERMIT.
HILL

SCOTTISH
HIGHLAND
CATTLE

ZEBRA

PHEASANTS

YAK

STAR OF
THE ZOO

SEA
LION

ELK

HAWK

FOOD

VULTURE

PICNIC
AREA

MAIN ENTRANCE

14

YOUR GUIDE TO TURTLE BACK ZOO

WHITE-TAILED DEER

TURKEY

EAGLE CAGE

LEOPARD

TORTOISERY

BARN

NURSERY

IRON HORSE

Eagle Rock Av.

Route 10

Pleasant Valley Way

Northfield Av.

Prospect Ave

Cherry Lane

ZOO

South Orange Av.

W. Tjark Reiss, the zoo's designer, created exhibits based on Hans Christian Anderson's nursery rhymes and other children's stories. Reiss had recently completed the architecture work for the children's zoo at Pittsburgh's Highland Park Zoo. As the Turtle Back Zoo continued to grow, Leonard Dreyfuss of United Outdoor Advertising added the Seal Pool, two large birdcages, and the Star of the Zoo exhibit. Dooner and Smith Chemical Co. contributed a home to the wise horned owl. Carteret Savings Bank gave Turtle Back its trademark, the Tortoisry. Over the years, several of these exhibits, such as the sea lion pool and Tortoisry, have been modified, but they remain. Some, such as the Cheese Wedge, Pig, and Okky exist only in photographs, and others, like the House of Cards and the Old Woman in a Shoe, are gone without a trace.

The Turtle Back Zoo was designed with child appeal in mind. Everything from drinking fountains to the coin telephones in nursery land–type sentry boxes were set up at levels convenient to children. The entrance and administration buildings resembled an Old English country village like those found in Hans Christian Anderson stories.

In 1963, the focus of the seasonal zoo was children. Exhibits were designed primarily for the younger ones using nursery-rhyme themes such as the Old Lady in the Shoe, Mother Goose, and Humpty Dumpty. Prairie dogs occupied a castle, and a South American rodent (capybara) lived in the Swiss Cheese Wedge.

These youngsters are leaving the Mayflower and entering the Children's Zoo. The pool around the ship housed a large variety of native and exotic waterfowl. The stone frog, visible on the left, was one of a number of similar-sized stone animals found throughout the zoo.

Two of the iconic structures from the zoo's opening were the New England Farm Barn and the Mayflower. The barn, shown here under construction, originally housed a variety of domestic animals that would be found on an early American family farm. The foundation for the Mayflower (foreground) was approximately 36 feet, or one-third the size of the ship that brought the Pilgrims to Plymouth, Massachusetts.

A Turtle Back Zoo postcard shows visitors on the Mayflower, which served as the entrance to the Children's Zoo. They would walk across a gangplank, pass through the ship, and exit through a set of stairs in the stern of the ship.

This view of the New England Farm Barn in the Children's Zoo shows the outdoor animal stalls, Rabbit Village, and turtle tables for the younger visitors to sit at. The bowsprit of the Mayflower can be seen on the far right, and the telephone booths and entrance are visible through the trees.

This small replica of a style of barn common in New England housed Shetland ponies and other barnyard creatures, such as sheep and calves. In the foreground of the photograph is the goose and tortoise paddock. This exhibit was filled with Canada, Emperor, Egyptian, and Greylag geese and Cameroon dwarf goats, but the main attraction was the 250-plus-pound Aldabra tortoises.

The silo on the barn was never used as an exhibit, but it helped the zoo visitor understand the simplicity and functionality of agriculture architecture. Winter is one of the least-attended times for the zoo, but it can also be the most enjoyable time for a visit. Peaceful scenes like this one are not often seen by the average summer zoo visitor.

The Howard Savings Bank built a prodigious pink "piggybank" for the display of tropical birds. The collection of birds in "the pig" included a beautiful Andean Cock-of-the-rock, the national bird of Peru. At one point, the enclosure contained Asiatic monkeys called macaques, which are related to baboons.

As the animal collection grew, the need arose for a dedicated space to care for the animals. Shown here is the Animal Care Center. The interior had a tile floor for easy cleaning and an office for animal care staff. In the mid-1970s, the animal care function outgrew this space, and the Animal Care Center became the Tortoisry, used to house the zoo's growing animal collection.

From the first days of the zoo, peacocks have been a common sight, roaming free on the grounds. They are adept at avoiding the close approaches of curious children during the day, and at night they will roost 20 to 30 feet in the trees. Peacocks will frequently enter other animal enclosures, such as the prairie dog castle, and help themselves to food.

Every storybook land needs a castle, and the one at Turtle Back Zoo was inhabited by prairie dogs. A group of black-tailed prairie dogs was imported from Texas and housed in a castle in the Children's Zoo. The prairie dogs would tunnel in the soil below the castle or climb on the ramparts to bask in the sun.

Although feeding animals is discouraged in most zoos nowadays, the young visitor in this photograph is enjoying feeding a prairie dog. Note the raised metal trim on top of the wall, intended to keep people from sitting on the wall or getting too close to the animals. The free-roaming peacocks would occasionally jump into the castle to steal food.

One of the more interesting exhibits in the original Children's Zoo was Okky the Jolly Octopus. Okky went through a number of changes during his stay. Initially, children could walk through his body, on both sides of which were aquariums. The tanks initially had piranha and arowana. After the walk-through was closed, double-crested cormorants that had been housed in the pool surrounding Okky used his body as a nesting area.

Starting as the home of Okky the Jolly Octopus, this exhibit had fish tanks inside that children could access across a bridge. A giant Asian softshell turtle can be seen in the pool. The bridge was later removed. After Okky was removed, the space became a seabird pool, housing one of the country's largest collections of cormorants. In 1978, the pool was rebuilt and deepened for alligators. (Courtesy of Brint Spencer.)

In the zoo's second year, Okky's pool was home to a harbor seal. Haul-out platforms were attached to the top of Okky's tentacles, and the seal could swim between the tentacles. The water around Okky held ducks and cormorants in addition to the seal.

One of the appealing aspects about the zoo's location at South Mountain was the wooded area. Exhibits were built under the trees, and the walkways were often composed of dirt or mulch, giving the zoo a comfortable and rustic feel. This natural tone was part of the vision that W. Tjark Reiss had for the zoo.

Chickens are an important part of most farmyards. Banty Town is where visitors could find fancy breeds of bantam chickens, primarily silkie and gray bantams. Many Japanese breeders specialized in unique and different-looking chickens, primarily for show. The silkie and gray breeds were Japanese developments.

Part of the excitement of the Children's Zoo was the circus-themed squirrel monkey exhibit. Bright reds and yellows made this exhibit immediately noticeable despite its location in the back of the Children's Zoo. The squirrel monkeys, crowd favorites, remained in the animal collection until 2009.

The Turtle Back Zoo opened with a storybook theme, and most of the animals in the Children's Zoo were farm animals. The Three Little Pigs was an important contributor to that theme. The pigs in this exhibit were young domestic pigs on loan from local farmers. Each year, the zoo would acquire piglets, lambs, calves, and goat kids from farms in New Jersey and Pennsylvania. At the end of the season, when the zoo closed, these animals were returned to the farms they came from.

This souvenir postcard shows many of the iconic features of the Children's Zoo as well as the zoo entrance and the South Mountain Reservation across the parking lot. The image offers a rare glimpse of the small yellow building called the Cheese Wedge. A window in the exhibit would typically house rodents. (Courtesy of Brint Spencer.)

A $5,000 gift was made by the Alice and Leonard Dreyfuss Foundation to be used for a Star of the Week display, which would feature a different exhibit of animals and birds each week. The Turtle Back Zoo had a close working relationship with the Terry-Lou Zoo in Scotch Plains, New Jersey, and many of the rotating animals came from there. This cage was later renamed the Star of the Zoo. Over the years, it housed baboons, leopards, capybaras, and baby tapirs.

In 1966, the Dreyfuss Advertising firm donated the funds to build a 13,000-gallon sea lion exhibit. When it opened, the pool had three female sea lions. With the exception of a small haul-out area, visitors were able to encircle the entire exhibit. Originally, a small bridge (seen here) went across the pool.

Feeding time at the zoo is a perennial favorite. As seen here, the sea lion exhibit usually drew a crowd when the animals were being fed. Sea lions are fed a diet of mixed fish, often including capelin, herring, mackerel, and squid. Depending on the season and the individual's size, a sea lion can eat 20 to 30 pounds of fish each day.

Part of the allure of many Turtle Back Zoo exhibits was how close the visitor could get to the animals. Here, a young California sea lion is seen with visitors. The pool had two haul-out areas: this small one, adjacent to the visitors, and a larger one at the opposite end of the pool, where the sea lions could get away from the crowds when they chose.

Volunteers from the Erie-Lackawanna Railroad laid one mile of track for the zoo's 24-inch-gauge railroad. The train leaves the station inside the zoo and runs a small loop through a Norway spruce forest. It then exits the zoo and runs alongside the 115-acre reservoir formerly owned by the City of Orange. A loop at the end of the track returns the train to the zoo.

The zoo's original train was an S-24 Iron Horse by the Allan Herschell Company of North Tonawanda, New York. The Herschell Iron Horse was a popular small-gauge train until 1970, when the company was purchased by Chance Manufacturing of Wichita, Kansas. The original passenger cars had canvas tops. These were later replaced by fiberglass.

31

Each of the three-ton locomotives was run on a 60-horsepower, water-cooled engine. In tribute to the Erie-Lackawanna volunteers who laid the tracks, the Erie "E" was displayed on the side of the engine. Observant riders on the train will also see the trademark "E" carved into a large vertical rock shortly after leaving the station.

A ride on the train has been a family tradition since the zoo opened. In fact, many visitors head straight to the train station after they enter the zoo. Over the years, the station has seen several face-lifts. In 2013, as part of the zoo's 50th anniversary, the original tower clock (shown here) was replaced with a newer model featuring a lighted dial. Aged wooden siding was replaced, and a faux rock knee wall was installed.

The Eating House was the zoo's original café. Fast food and soda were sold inside, and there were indoor and outdoor dining areas. A picnic area served visitors who brought their own lunch. In 1985, this building was replaced by the new and expanded café.

Among the early residents of the Turtle Back Zoo were three Aldabra tortoises. During the zoo's first two seasons, the public was allowed to ride the tortoises, and today many of those visitors remember riding them. The tortoise shown here has the warning "Do Not Hand Feed" painted on the front of its shell so that riders would keep their fingers out of danger.

Two

The 1970s
The Role a Zoo Plays

In the simplest terms, a zoo is a place where animals live in captivity and are put on display for people to view. But, the role a zoo plays is far from simple. In most cases, a zoo's purpose can be categorized into four roles: conservation, research, family recreation, and education.

Conservation is achieved by zoos through endangered species captive-breeding programs. These are valuable to a species' survival. In many instances, an animal will be extinct in the wild, and the handful of surviving individuals will only exist in zoo facilities. Researchers at zoos can observe animal behavior, such as mating and nutrition choices. Zoos can share data to provide animals with the most appropriate habitats and adequate enrichment activities. These studies then offer information for the successful conservation of sustainable natural habitats. Not to be forgotten is that a zoo has to be fun and family friendly. Visitors to the zoo can be fully engaged just through the presence of the animals. Technology cannot create the same atmosphere of the zoo or entice the emotional bond made between a visitor and an animal.

The most important goal for zoos is to provide extensive educational opportunities, which is done in a variety of ways. More realistic exhibits depict flora and terrain typical of the species' native habitat. On the people side of the exhibit, interactive displays and large signs and pictures encourage visitors to take part in the learning experience.

In the 1970s, Turtle Back Zoo began the push toward expanding its already popular education division. The first step was the construction of the Leonard and Alice Dreyfuss Education Center. The formation of the not-for-profit Zoological Society of New Jersey helped fund further educational initiatives throughout the decade. A voter referendum in 1978 enacted a charter change in Essex County, replacing the autonomous Board of Park Commissioners with a new administration.

Construction began on the Leonard and Alice Dreyfuss Educational Center. The facility allowed the zoo to be open year-round. Alice Dreyfuss and the Dreyfuss foundation provided funds, matched by the county, to build the center. Completed in 1974, the education center provided a classroom for group visits, offices, exhibit space, and an animal nursery. The nursery is where on-site

animals and those used in outreach programming were kept. The zoo is now open year-round, weather permitting. The hours of operation are expanded in warmer months to accommodate larger crowds.

In July and August, Reptile Summer was featured in the Education Center. This was the only time of the year for visitors to see snakes that were usually kept "off-exhibit" in the animal nursery area. Sometimes an iguana from the West Orange High School Science Department was brought in for "Reptile Summer" in the Education Center.

The Zoological Society of New Jersey appropriated $2,450 in 1976 for a marine tide-pool tank to be placed in the Education Center. Quickly becoming an integral part of the zoo's education program, the tank gave visitors a "hands-on" familiarity with New Jersey's aquatic inhabitants. The marine tank would be refilled for the summer months with starfish, hermit crabs, snails, and horseshoe crabs (seen here being held by zoo educator Vince Sharp).

From the opening Sunday, when 10,000 people came to the zoo, and to the present time, the zoo has been a popular destination. A full parking lot is a common sight in the summer. As zoo visitation increased, adjacent fields and the archery range were used as overflow parking. A three-level parking deck was added in 2004. Its capacity has since been exceeded, so a second deck is being designed. Construction is set to begin in 2014. (Courtesy of D. Pierson.)

By 1973, more than 15,000 schoolchildren were visited by the zoo's traveling education programs; another 36,000 saw an education program at the zoo while on class trips. Arriving at the zoo complex, schoolchildren can see South Mountain Arena (pictured here). The original rink was completed in 1958 to provide year-round skating and non-skating activities to the general public. A second rink was added in 1983, and in 1986 South Mountain Arena became the official practice and training facility of the New Jersey Devils.

Many school groups attended scheduled programs led by zoo educators. These programs transformed a zoo visit from a field trip into an educational experience. Educators wore green-and-white checkered shirts to distinguish themselves from the Zooettes, in their red-and-white checkered shirts. Here, Lillian Dierdle presents a ball python.

Many of today's moms and dads, now with young children of their own, have memories of visiting the zoo as a child. Helen Friermuth was one of the first educators hired by the zoo. Educators were responsible for the daily care of the animals they used in presentations. Friermuth was devoted to the animals and the children she encountered during her time at the zoo. Resting comfortably on her shoulder is a ring-tailed cat.

Giving greater importance to the role of education following the 1960s, zoos provided the critical function of connecting people to nature by engaging them with living animals. The hope was that these special experiences would create lasting memories that would in turn foster environmentally conscious behavior. Here, Michael Kane presents an African hedgehog.

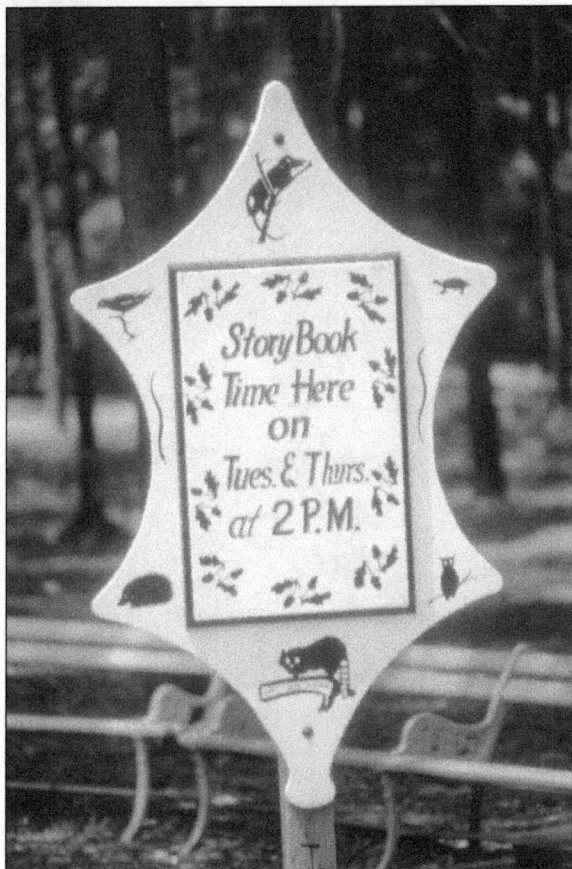

Story Book
Time Here
on
Tues. & Thurs.
at 2 P.M.

Storybook time took place at 2:00 p.m. every Tuesday and Thursday. Moms and their young children would gather in an open area near the train entrance. Wood logs and turtle-shaped tables served as resting places for families to listen to a short story. Read by an education staff member, the story always featured a live animal friend. A brass bell was rung to let children know that story time was about to begin.

The zoo's education programs continued to grow throughout the 1970s; these were held on and off zoo grounds. A collection of easy-to-handle animals was maintained for these programs. Here, a bush baby is presented. The familiar gingham shirts worn by the presenters were donated by Bamberger's Department Stores, based in Newark, New Jersey. (Courtesy of George Kemper.)

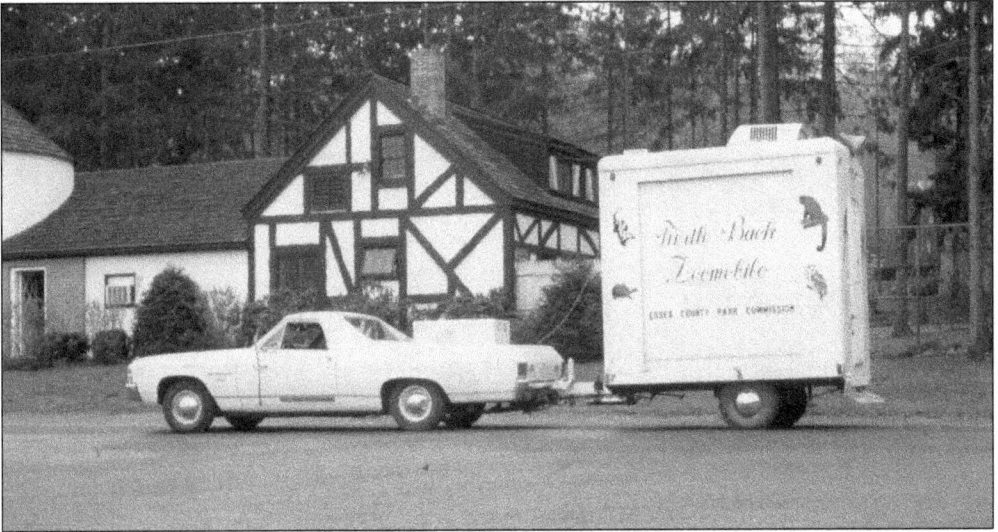

Turtle Back Zoo's commitment to outreach conservation education had its beginning with the Zoomobile, which was taken to county and municipal parks programs. Live animals were also taken to schools, libraries, and scout programs and used for in-zoo classroom programs. By the 1980s, there were four full-time education staff members. Only a few of the larger zoos in the county employed that many educators at the time. Turtle Back Zoo was in the forefront of this shift in a zoo's purpose, from entertainment to education.

The ABC House acted as a base for the travelling zoo programs, which had been started in 1965 with one zoo employee and eight animals. The presenters loaded the animals into the Zoomobile, drove to the destination, dropped the back of the van, and conducted their programs. The initial 1971 season with the Zoomobile was considered a huge success. The mobile unit visited over 9,000 adults and adolescents throughout the county park system.

Outreach mall exhibits were presented two or three times a year during the 1970s and 1980s. The exhibits' main purpose was public relations, but the education staff and animal keepers also emphasized conservation awareness. Mall exhibits usually lasted for three days and required detailed logistical planning and staffing. Some animals needed larger caging. Turtle Back Zoo held exhibitions at the Livingston, Willowbrook, Bergen, Riverside, and Rockaway Malls. At the opening celebrations of the Rockaway Mall, the zoo introduced to the public its Siberian tiger cub, Feelings.

This Siberian tiger cub is having some quality enrichment time with zoo educator Vince Sharp. Educational talks conducted at a zoo exhibit are known as "keeper talks." Sharp would teach zoo visitors about the tiger's endangered status and how, at times, it becomes necessary for animals to be hand-raised by keepers. This tiger had been rejected by his mother. Keepers acted as surrogates until the animal was old enough to care for itself or until the keeper had too many tears in their clothes! At that time, one-on-one keeper/animal contact was slowly reduced. Training sessions and keeper talks were then moved outside the exhibit space for safety. Cougars, bobcats, and wolves are just a few of the animals that have also been hand-raised at the zoo.

This type of concrete and chain-link exhibit space could be found at zoos throughout the country in the early 1970s. They were easy for keepers to clean, and animals could be safely moved from them when needed. Such spaces provided both horizontal and vertical movement, but it was limited. An animal's health was not compromised, but the visitor's perception was that the exhibits were too confining. Today, cat species are exhibited in spacious, naturalistic enclosures. Visitors perceive the creatures not as caged animals but as members of a species in their habitat.

This exhibit had four enclosures. One housed Cleopatra, a spotted leopard (above). Although the space had two types of protective fencing, visitors could still get very close to the large cats. Cleo was named so because records showed the famous Egyptian queen kept spotted leopards in captivity. Another resident was the spotted leopard Brutus (below). His melanistic covering made him look very different than Cleo, but his "hidden" spots could be seen in the right light. The other two enclosures held Buster, a Siberian tiger, and Yeti, a snow leopard.

Four North American river otters were born at the Turtle Back Zoo in early 1972. They made their public debut in May. Otter births in captivity in the 1970s were uncommon, and four surviving pups was a rare occurrence. The father had been separated from the family and was held in another exhibit. In 1985, the zoo held the first otter captive-breeding symposium, which brought zoo professionals from around the country to discuss otter management.

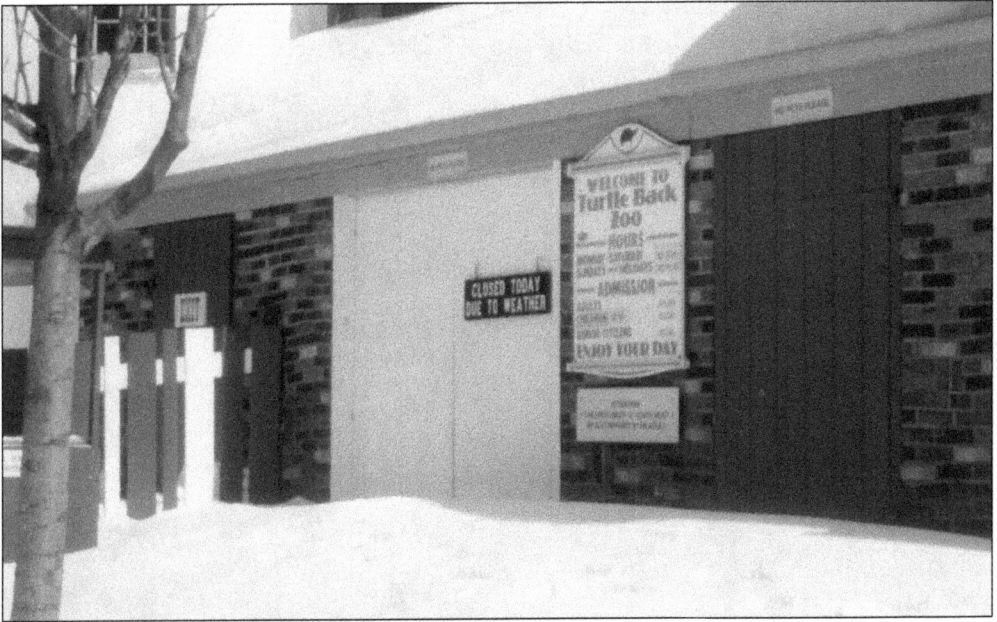

In the early 1970s, the zoo became a year-round facility. It encouraged people to visit in the winter, but there were days when Mother Nature won out. On such occasions, the zoo would be closed for the safety of the animals and public. Since the zoo is located on the side of South Mountain, the topography presents interesting challenges to the visitors, the animals, and the zookeepers, who work regardless of the weather.

Dr. John Devine was the first veterinarian hired by the Turtle Back Zoo. He had not always planned on being an animal doctor, and he started veterinary school later in life than most of his colleagues. He is shown here examining a camel.

As the zoo expanded, the animal collection changed. The farm barn that had housed domestic animals when the zoo opened now held up to three South America tapirs (shown here). These large herbivores had indoor and outdoor stalls. A pool was built into one of the outdoor stalls to accommodate the tapirs' semi-aquatic lifestyle.

Zookeeper Sue Mitschke grooms a South American tapir in the outdoor paddocks of the farm barn. Mitschke would go on to hold numerous positions at the zoo before retiring as the purchasing agent in 2012. She was the longest-tenured staff member in Turtle Back Zoo history.

The Children's Zoo was a special place, where children got to experience a variety of animals on their own and in ways that excited them. Here, a young visitor and a rhea check each other out. Children were allowed to feed many of the animals in the Children's Zoo.

Okky became the seabird exhibit, housing five different species of cormorant. The zoo now had one of the most complete cormorant collections in the country, including great, double-crested, pelagic, guanay, and olivaceous. The two great cormorants were imported from the Tokyo Zoo. Cormorants built nests under Okky's structure.

Originally part of the Children's Zoo and labeled as a termite mound, the Bat Cave was located between the alligator pool and the otter exhibit in the early 1970s. It housed 15 lesser spear-nosed bats from Central and South America. These bats, which feed on fruit, are four inches long and have an eight-inch wingspan. The exhibit had a reversed light cycle, so the lights were off during the day and on at night.

Bats were housed in the Bat Cave as well as the Tortoisry. In early April 1988, zookeeper Allen Foust found a baby bat that had fallen from its mother. Not wanting to take a chance that it might fall again if returned, he decided to hand-raise it. Named Belfrey, she was hung on Foust's T-shirt. For the next six weeks, they were never apart. Belfrey had to be fed every two hours until she was two weeks old! Penguins can be seen in the foreground residing in Okky's pool.

One of the more interesting sights was a monkey exhibit, consisting of two towers with a rope in between. A spider monkey or woolly monkey was secured to the rope by a leash around the monkey's waist. The monkey could move back and forth across the rope. Each of the towers provided food, water, and shade. Seen in the background is the Pig, which housed a variety of tropical birds and to the left is a refreshment and animal food stand.

Children's birthday parties have been popular since the early days of the zoo. The party room was located on the second floor of the right turret (when looking at the zoo from the front). Children got to eat their birthday cake at a large green, wooden, turtle-shaped table.

Well over 100 years ago, zoo directors began using Groundhog Day as a public-relations event to promote their institutions. Turtle Back Zoo joined this tradition and introduced "Chuck the Woodchuck," referred to formally as "Woodrow K. Chuck," to compete with Northeast celebrities like Punxsutawney Phil, Pothole Pete, and Staten Island Chuck in weather prognostication. Not a lot of visitors come to the zoo on February 2 to see the groundhog prediction firsthand, but millions listen for it on drive-time radio or view it on morning and evening news programs. Shown above is Channel 7 reporter Pablo Guzman in 1977. Chuck is sending a letter via an opossum stating that he had seen his shadow and was going back to sleep. Below, zookeeper Sue Mitschke is getting a direct prognostication from Essex Ed.

Turtle Back Zoo records show that Mr. Chuck and his successors, Lacey and Essex Ed, have consistently been the area's best forecasters. Learning from some of the best, Essex Ed "interned" for a year at the Punxsutawney Zoo before making his home in New Jersey. Ed continues to interpret the signs of spring yearly from his home at Turtle Back next to the black bear exhibit.

At the end of every spring, it was necessary for the sheep to be sheered of their heavy winter costs. This was a great opportunity for a special event. In exchange for the wool, a professional sheep sheerer would trim the sheep for the zoo. Visitors were able to observe the sheering process. What appears to be a crazy haircut is done in a couple minutes, resulting in a much cooler and happier sheep. Around the farm, there were also demonstrations of carding, spinning, and weaving. Today, this tradition lives on with the sheering taking place on Memorial Day.

The Senior Art Show, held by the Parks Commission, is still a staple event of Essex County every year, although its location has changed. At the one-day event, submitted paintings were hung along fencing throughout the zoo for visitors to enjoy, while different sculptures were displayed inside the Education Center. Ribbons were awarded to the top winners, judged by the First Mountain Crafters. The art show was the final event of Senior Citizen Week at Turtle Back Zoo. From September 18 to 24, 1972, the zoo entrance fee was reduced from $1 to 25¢. Guided tours, touch-and-feel programs, a peek at the inside of the zoo's operations, train rides, picnics, and special displays awaited seniors who joined in the festivities.

Peafowl are probably the most photographed birds at the zoo. Free-roaming peacocks (male) and peahens (female) have always been a big attraction. In early spring, peacocks begin their courting displays, fanning out their signature feathers to flaunt to peahens, glass windows, and the occasional visitor. Catching a photograph of this behavior is a delight.

Occasionally, the zoo's peafowl would leave the security of the zoo and stroll out the gate. One summer day, this bird wandered into the South Mountain Ice Arena (now Cody Arena) and interrupted the summer ice-skating lessons. The bird was then ushered back in the direction of the zoo.

The zoo has always exhibited an interesting and diverse collection of birds. Zoo director Richard Ryan, with years of experience as an ornithologist, began to expand the number of bird species at the zoo. When Gretchen and Larry Rachlin tragically lost a son, his college fund provided a memorial to his love of nature: the Pheasant Aviary. The aviary featured four species of pheasant. In this photograph, a zookeeper moves a bird from one enclosure to another.

In addition to pheasants, a number of other birds were housed in the Pheasant Aviary. This white-crested laughing thrush is found in mountain forests of Southeast Asia. The laughing thrush is an active, boisterous species whose call sounds like laughter. This species would return to the zoo's Asian forest exhibit in the reptile house 40 years later.

A mile south of the zoo, within the South Mountain Reservation, was the Essex County Deer Paddock. This 20-acre refuge was home to a small herd of fallow deer. Daily animal care was provided by keepers at the zoo. Every few years, it was necessary to cull the herd. Surplus animals were sent to a large animal preserve in the Shenandoah Valley. This area is now the location of the South Mountain Reservation Dog Park.

Elk, or wapiti, is the second-largest member of the deer family and have long been associated with the Turtle Back Zoo. The zoo's herd was usually dominated by a single adult bull with a harem of two to four females. The bull's bugling was often heard echoing off of South Mountain on fall evenings. (Courtesy of Brint Spencer.)

61

During the fall rut, bull elk would become more aggressive, and there was a risk that they would injure the females during courtship and breeding bouts. One management strategy to reduce the risk of injury was to cut off the bull's rack. The animal was anesthetized and his eyes covered to help keep him calm. A wire saw was used to cut the antlers off. Once the antlers were removed, the bull would continue to court the females, but he would not be able to injure them.

Another interesting species housed at the zoo in the 1970s was the sitatunga. This African antelope has numerous adaptations for their semi-aquatic lifestyle. They have elongated hooves for moving through aquatic vegetation, and they can submerge themselves to avoid predators, keeping only their nostrils above water.

One of the most uncommon hoofstock species ever housed at the Turtle Back Zoo was the saiga. These antelope, listed as critically endangered, are now found only in the grassy steppe regions of Russia. The bulbous nose is believed to help warm the air when animals breathe during the harsh Russian winter. The males can be aggressive, and to keep them from injuring the females their horns are cut and tipped with rubber hoses.

Santa takes time out of his busy schedule to feed some of the whitetailed deer at the zoo. Santa has made many appearances at the zoo during the holidays so that children can personally present their Christmas lists. Over the years, the zoo has featured many deer species: whitetail deer, caribou, elk (red deer), sika, muntjac, and fallow deer.

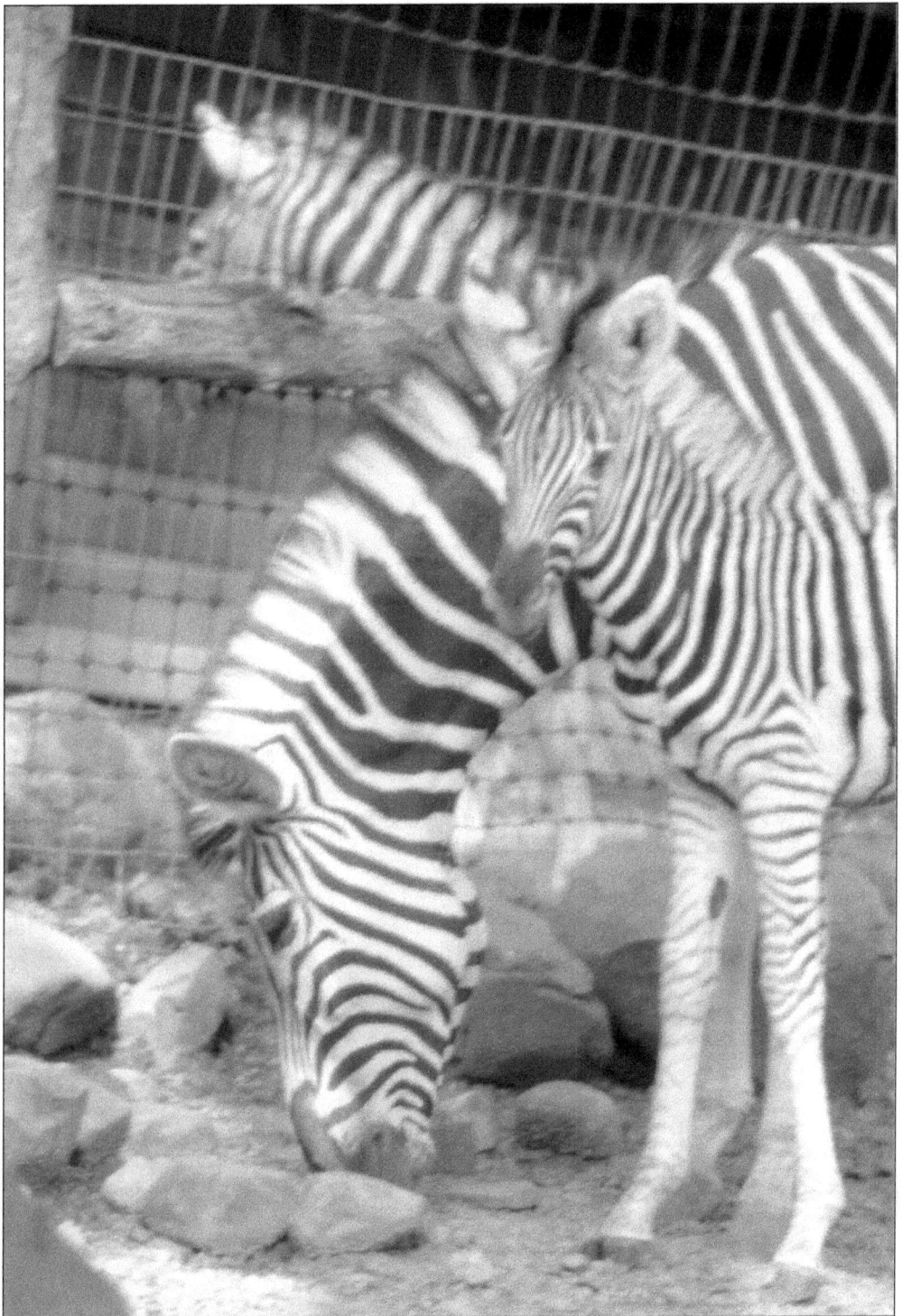

In 1973, the zoo's resident zebras, Zeke and Zizi, welcomed their first baby, Zelda, who was born on July 6. A new barn was built for camels and zebras two years later to accommodate the growing numbers. This barn is still used and today houses Scottish Highland cattle.

In the late 1960s and early 1970s, Paul Olsen (right) and Tony Lessa (left) found over 1,000 fossils, including a *Eubrontes giganteus* footprint, in the nearby Kidde stone quarry. The boys made a cast of the *Eubrontes* footprint and sent it to Pres. Richard Nixon. A portion of the quarry was donated to the Esssex County Park Commission, and in 1971 it was declared a National Natural Landmark. Olsen went on to earn a PhD in paleontology from Yale University. In 2013, the Turtle Back Zoo added a dinosaur-themed playground to the zoo.

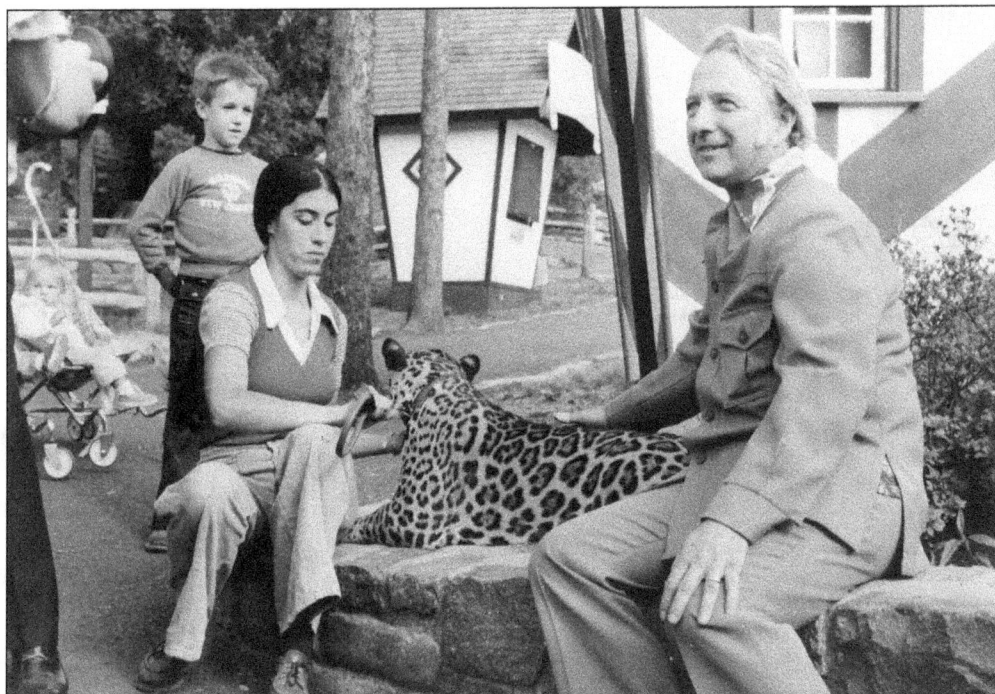

Richard Ryan (right) became zoo director in 1965 and served into the 1990s. He is seen here showing a jaguar. The zoo did not actually exhibit jaguars at this time. For certain special events, Frank Terry from the Terry Lou Zoo in Scotch Plains would bring unique animals from his collection. Many people remember Ryan as an accomplished ornithologist. During most of his directorship, he led weekly birding trips within northern and central New Jersey. He also led two or three trips a year to Central and South America.

Greg Toffic, the keeper of the zoo's extensive bird collection, would help director Ryan with bird walks. Toffic's interest in birds led him to further his career at a zoo in the Midwest. Eventually, he became curator of birds at the Woodland Park Zoo in Seattle, Washington. Toffic is seen here (second from the left) leading a group of bird enthusiasts in the early morning hours.

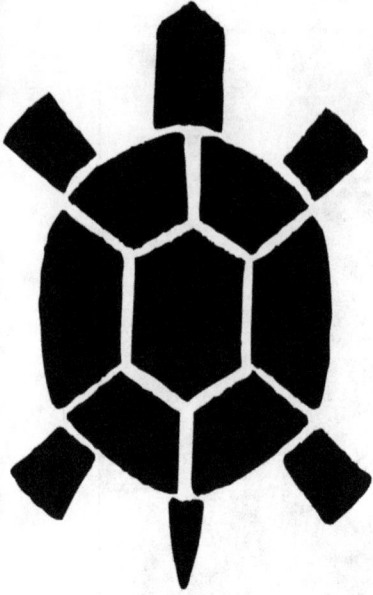

Zoological Society of New Jersey, Inc.

The Zoological Society of New Jersey, Inc., was started in 1973, a decade after the zoo opened, but it was not incorporated until April 15, 1975. Established as a nonprofit organization, the society acted as an advisory body for development as well as for educational and fundraising purposes of the Turtle Back Zoo. Monies raised through memberships, gifts, and grants are used to expand the zoo's animal collection and existing exhibits. This mission statement of the Zoological Society also includes promoting the general welfare of the zoo; financing new facilities, equipment, and acquisitions of animals; and stimulating public interest in the development and enjoyment of the Essex County Turtle Back Zoo and animals everywhere.

Over the years, the zoological society has initiated a number of successful fundraising activities. During its Paver Program, it sold more than 350 engraved paver stones, which are installed in the zoo's entrance pavilion. The society's biggest fundraiser, though, has been selling memberships. Among its many benefits, a membership allows unlimited free admittance to Turtle Back Zoo for an entire year.

There were over 80 species of turtle in the zoo collection, including every species of New Jersey turtle. As the collection grew, there was a need for a place to display and manage them. The Animal Infirmary transitioned into the Tortoisry, becoming the home for the zoo's expanding turtle collection.

In 1968, Carteret Savings & Loan provided the funding for the Tortoisry exhibit as a gift to the people of Essex County. This exhibit was dedicated to the memory of M. Wilfred Rice, Essex park commissioner and president of the bank. Zoo staff was involved in the design and construction of the Tortoisry.

A pool on one end of the exhibit provided underwater viewing to allow visitors to better see the aquatic turtles. This pool led into a waterfall, which cascaded to the floor of the exhibit. Large skylights allowed natural light to enter for the benefit of plants. The concrete rocks and the trees had planter pockets for plants to grow throughout.

Aldabra tortoises were in the collection for years. For the first couple of years, visitors were allowed to ride on the tortoises, and many current visitors still remember riding them as children. In the winter, the giant tortoises were moved into the Tortoisry exhibit so they could still be viewed by the public. In 2011, Aldabra tortoises were brought back to the zoo and housed in the South American Yard.

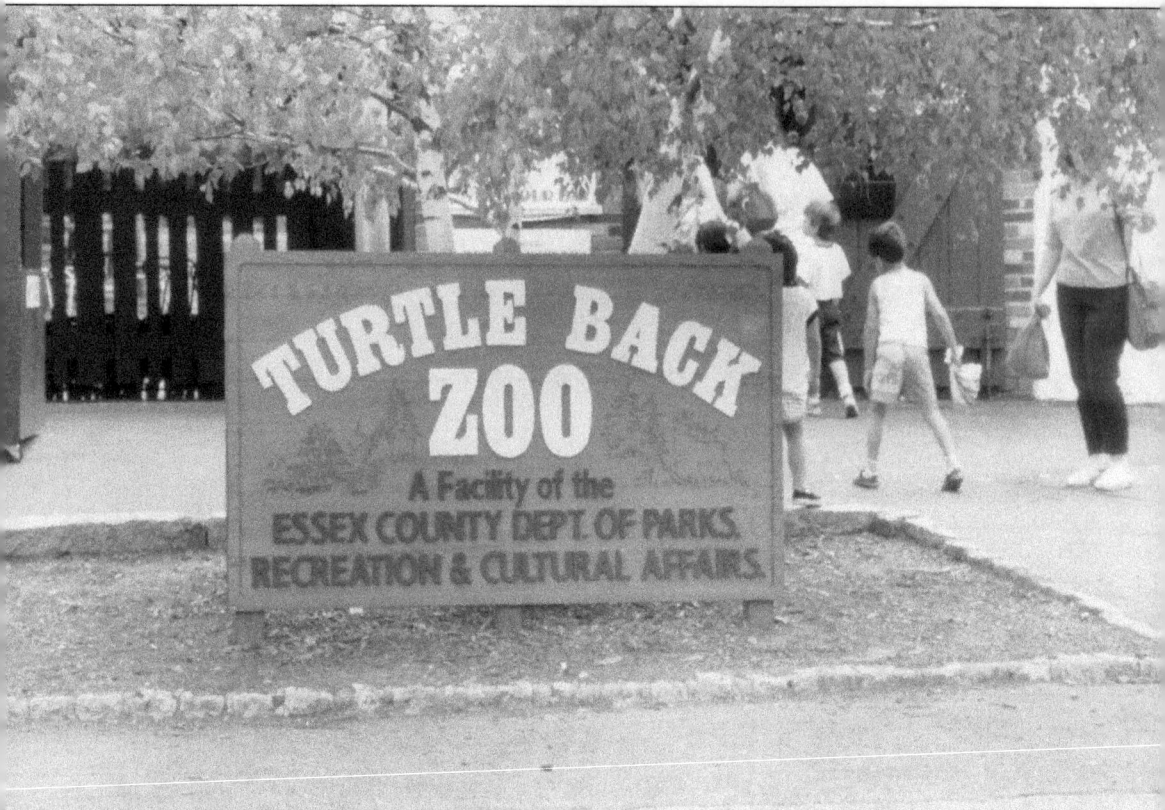

A voter referendum in 1978 enacted a charter change in Essex County, replacing the autonomous Board of Park Commissioners with a new administration. A county executive, Peter Shapiro, was elected. He in turn appointed Daniel Bogan as county administrator and William Scalzo as director of parks, recreation, and cultural affairs.

Three

THE 1980S
EXPANSION

The 1980s was all about growth for Turtle Back Zoo. Phase one of the New Jersey Wild master plan continued to move forward with the ground breaking of Wolf Woods by the end of the decade. Increased visitor attendance, especially school groups, meant enlarging the gathering areas around the zoo. An amphitheater would provide a larger area to accommodate the hundreds of individuals who gathered for educational programming.

The start of the docent program, then sponsored by the Zoological Society of New Jersey, gave the zoo a large volunteer base from which to staff education stations throughout zoo grounds and assist with animal handling at public presentations. These increased opportunities for visitor-docent encounters made the visit a more memorable experience.

These interactions with visitors gave zoo staff insight into the common zoo consumer, allowing zoo officials to further expand and refine the zoo experience. Visitors in turn got a personal zoo experience that they would remember for years to come.

Special events flourished during this decade. Some events, like the antique car show, were recurrent favorites, while new events, such as the Pumpkin Patch and Rat-and-Bat Night, began to gain momentum. The Zoological Society of New Jersey began a new fundraiser with the Adopt-an-Animal program. While adoption really means sponsoring, this program continues to fill a necessary and vital role at Turtle Back Zoo by helping in the feeding, care, and maintenance of the animal collection.

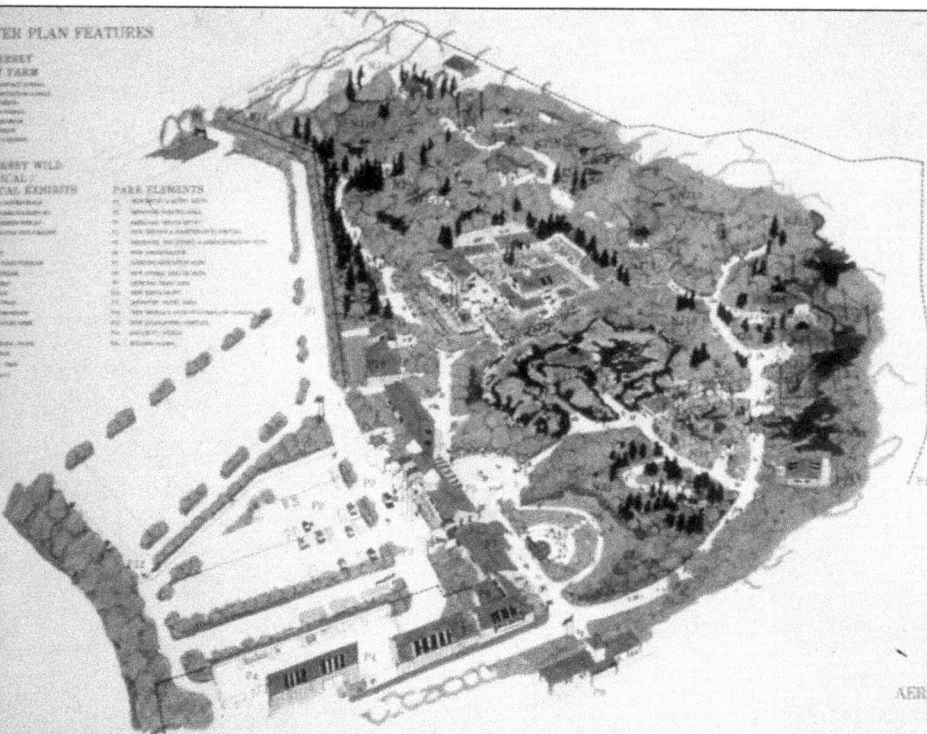

AERIAL SKETCH LOOKING NORTH

TURTLE BACK ZOO MASTER PLA

DEPT. of PARKS, RECREATION & CULTURAL AFF
CITY OF WEST ORANGE, ESSEX COUNTY, NEW JE
JONES & JONES   COE &

Further development of phase one of the master plan, New Jersey Wild, was to include an Animal Food Complex, owl cages, reconstruction of the seabird exhibit and small mammal exhibit, and surveying of a future site for the wolf exhibit. In 1986, the Turtle Back Zoo docent newsletter, *The Bugle*, stated, "For 'New Jersey Wild' to become a reality it will be necessary to fully involve the region's private and corporate communities for support. Zoological parks are living museums. They provide a vital interaction between the human and other living things. They offer people the chance to experience and wonder at the astonishing diversity of life. Our generation and future generations need to understand and come to value the human animal's relationship to nature. If we can develop positive attitudes about conservation, we can save some animals and their habitats, and in so doing we may be able to save ourselves."

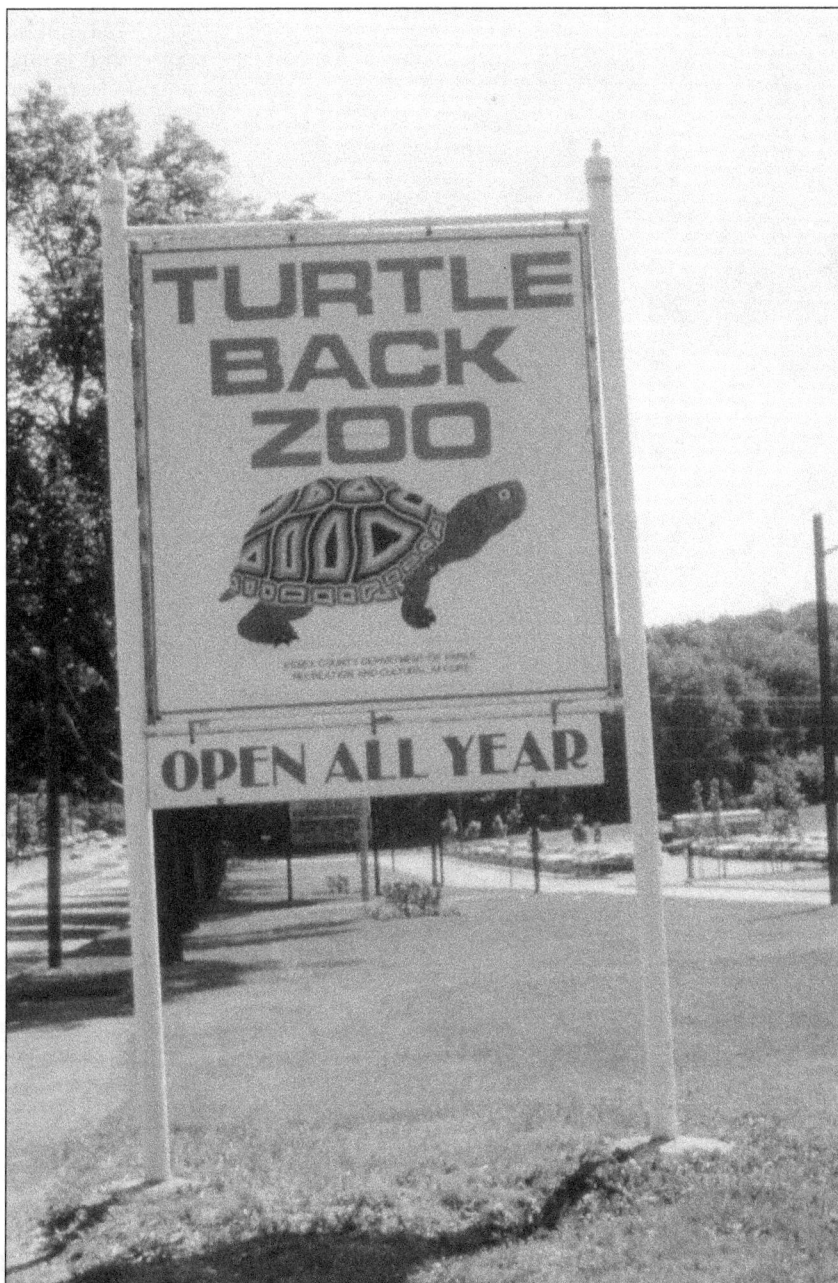

On Saturday, June 4, 1988, the zoo celebrated its 25th anniversary. County officials were on hand to help honor the zoo and ceremonially open the zoo for the next 25 years. Joining county executive Nicholas R. Amato at the opening ceremonies were president of the Board of Chosen Freeholders, Thomas Giblin; director of the Department of Parks, Recreation and Cultural Affairs, Carmine E. Capone; Freeholder Carmine P. Casciano; and zoo director Richard Ryan. Paul Meade, curator of the animal collection, and James Hunsinger, animal keeper, received certificates honoring their 25 years of service to the zoo. The weekend festivities continued into Sunday, featuring clowns, balloons, commemorative sweatshirts, bumper stickers, a special moon bounce, and live music.

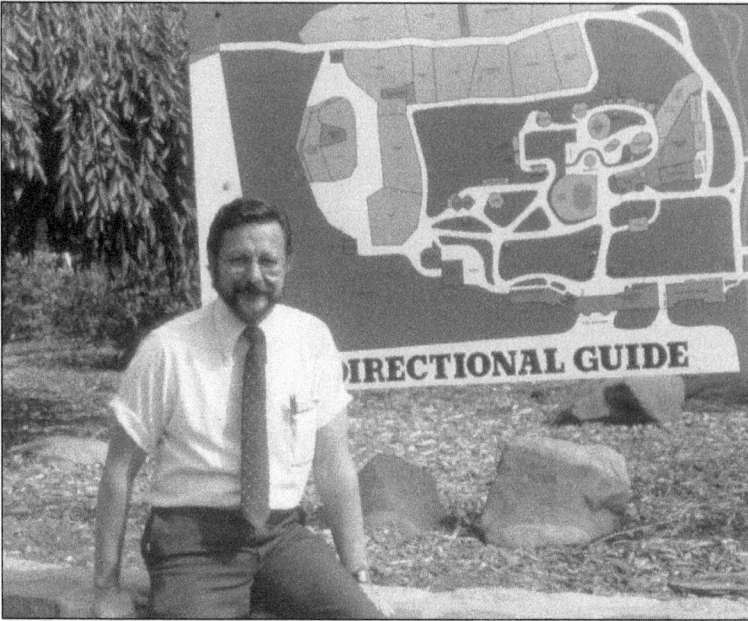

Assistant director Boris Lyzak, sitting in front of a zoo directional guide at the front entrance, was part of the zoo throughout the 1970s and 1980s. The zoo grew in leaps and bounds during Lyzak's tenure in no small part because of his efforts. He worked closely with the education staff on special events and with keeper staff on animal husbandry.

Looking out the window of the Education Center's animal holding area, education animal ambassador, a tawny frogmouth, checks out a roaming peafowl. An opportunity arose to conveniently house the zoo's education animal collection when the Education Center was built. Large windows on one side provided natural light to the animals that were mostly used for educational programming. A secondary benefit was that visitors could view some of their favorite education animals. If this photograph is any indication, the zoo's peafowl seemed to get some enjoyment out of this feature as well.

During the 1980s, the number of school-group visits increased dramatically. A place to accommodate large groups for animal programs was hard to find; it was time to build an amphitheater. The county and the Zoological Society of New Jersey provided the funds, and the structure was built by 1987. In 1988, the Orange-West Orange chapter of UNICO National, an Italian American service organization, made a generous donation of a portable sound system for use during programming and other zoo events.

On sunny days at the zoo, educator Vince Sharp would be on stage with a microphone, live animals, and "biofacts," teaching a sea of visitors sprawled out on the amphitheater lawn. Over his 33 years as education curator, Sharp spent thousands of hours on the amphitheater stage, having children "repeat after me." Upon his retirement in 2011, the zoo dedicated the amphitheater in his name. The plaque reads, "The Vince Sharp Wildlife Education Amphitheater—Dedicated to a Lifelong Educator and Friend to Animals and their Habitats."

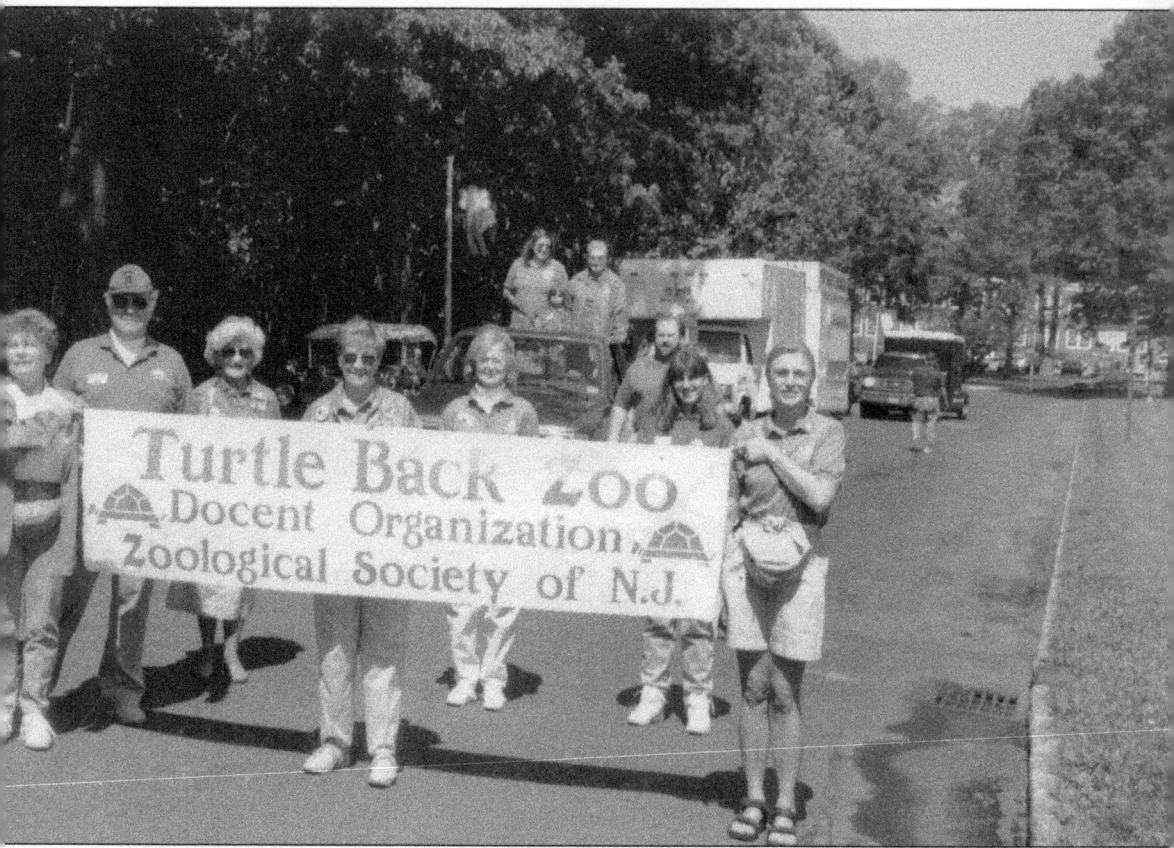

The docent organization at Turtle Back Zoo began in the fall of 1984. The first graduating class had 23 people. In the beginning, the Zoological Society of New Jersey sponsored the docent program. The charter class was taught by the curator. There were few guidelines available, and at the end of the training the new docents were launched onto the zoo grounds to teach visitors about animals. In 1997, the docents became the docents of Essex County Turtle Back Zoo, sponsored by the Essex County Department of Parks, Recreation and Cultural Affairs.

The *Bugle* newsletter best described the zoo docents: "But WHO exactly are these Docents? Docents range in age from people in their early twenties to retirees. Most come from Essex, Morris, and Union counties; however, Hudson, Bergen, Somerset, Passaic, and Middlesex are also represented. Talk to a Docent and you might be talking to a lawyer, nurse, homemaker, teacher, artist, fireman, policeman, bookkeeper, someone who works for a large corporation or someone who is self-employed. Docents, in other words, are a diverse group of people with one common trait; a LOVE and CONCERN for animals, plus an interest in learning more about these animals and an enthusiasm to share this knowledge with zoo visitors." Docents spend many hours greeting buses and "people organizing."

On July 12, 1987, the National Association of County Park and Recreation Officials (NACPRO) presented their Friends of Parks and Recreation Award to the Docent Organization of the Zoological Society of New Jersey. Only a couple of years old at this point, the docent organization already had over 70 members donating their free time to the zoo.

Docent Alice shows a leopard skull to visitors. In the background is Brutus, a melanistic spotted leopard. Many people know these majestic animals as "panthers" due to the Tarzan movies. Docents used skulls, termed "biofacts," as interactive educational tools for visitors to create connections that would last beyond their visit to the zoo.

Myrtle the Turtle was a natural fit to become the mascot of the Turtle Back Zoo. Myrtle has seen one makeover during her time at Turtle Back and has always been a crowd pleaser. Everyone wants to pose for a photograph or give a high-five or a hug when they catch Myrtle at a zoo event or waving in one of the local parades.

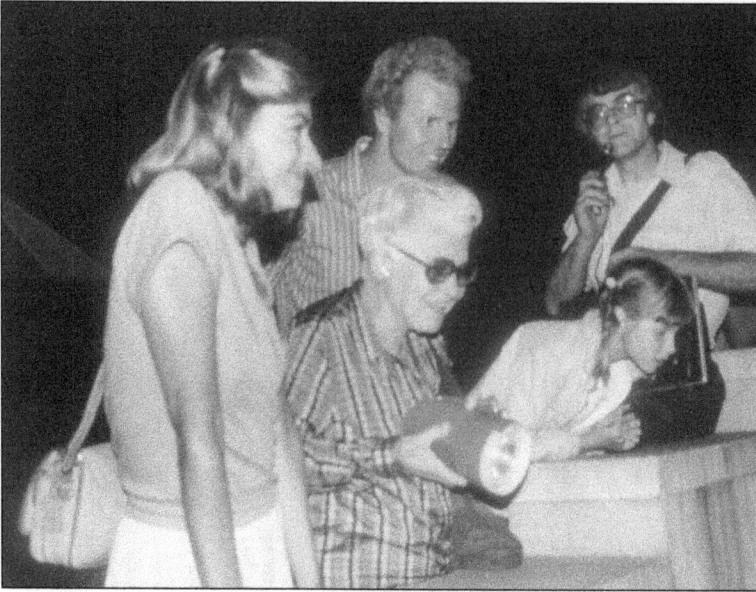

Night Moves is a nighttime guided tour of the zoo. Visitors come to the zoo with flashlights and enthusiasm for the chance to see the zoo in a different light. Tours focus on animal behavior and adaptations necessary to survive in the dark. Originally led by education staff, in 1988 docents began to lead the tours.

Barbara Dyer is seen here holding the Education Center's program opossum O-Feel-Ya. Dyer was an educator, animal keeper, and special events coordinator. In the background is an official voting machine. For many years in the 1980s, visitors could vote on this machine for their favorite zoo animal. The real reason for voting, however, was to allow visitors to familiarize themselves with the more general voting process and to help remove the fear of using the machine. Studies had revealed that this fear had kept people from voting. The program was conducted in cooperation with the League of Women Voters.

For many years during the 1970s and 1980s, for one day only, antique automobile owners were invited to the zoo to showcase their meticulously restored cars. Here, Pat Frederick stands by a 1940 Mercury Convertible owned by George Fisher of West Orange. The hood ornament is a Turtle Back Zoo falcon. About 50 cars were on display. (Courtesy of Boris Lyzak.)

One draw of the car show is the 60 years of automobile history that could be viewed with one walk around the parking lot. Stories were exchanged, as particular vehicles brought memories of first cars and first dates. The 1976 car show had three divisions: antique (predating 1929), production cars (from 1930 on), and classics (specialty cars). The Animal Services Building is in the back right of the image.

The fall season is an especially busy time at zoos. The return of school means busloads of school groups on weekdays. Cooler weather brings droves of families on the weekends. Even for visitors who had come to the zoo earlier in the year, the fall foliage throughout the surrounding South Mountain Reservation resulted in a distinctive new experience on the train ride and in the overall visit.

Making the most of comfortable outdoor temperatures and already high attendance numbers, zoos plan many special events for October. For many zoos, Halloween-inspired activities are the largest event of the year. At Turtle Back Zoo, the first annual Pumpkin Patch special event, in 1988, featured pumpkin sales and decorating, music, and puppet shows. Subsequent years saw added activities, such as costume contests and a not-so-spooky train ride.

In the early 1980s, the zoo decided to host a mischief night special event. Halloween eve was chosen for the event, providing parents with an opportunity for a safe Halloween experience that even a teenager could be talked into attending. The event was named Rat-and-Bat Night, with the idea that visitors' misconceptions about bats and rats as "bad animals" could, with a little education, be changed. After the first year, the education staff realized that no one was interested in being educated when dressed up, in the dark, in a zoo. Magic shows, costume contests, and scary train rides along a dark lake deep into the zoo's surrounding forest became the focus of an event that provided an extended-family experience for thousands of visitors.

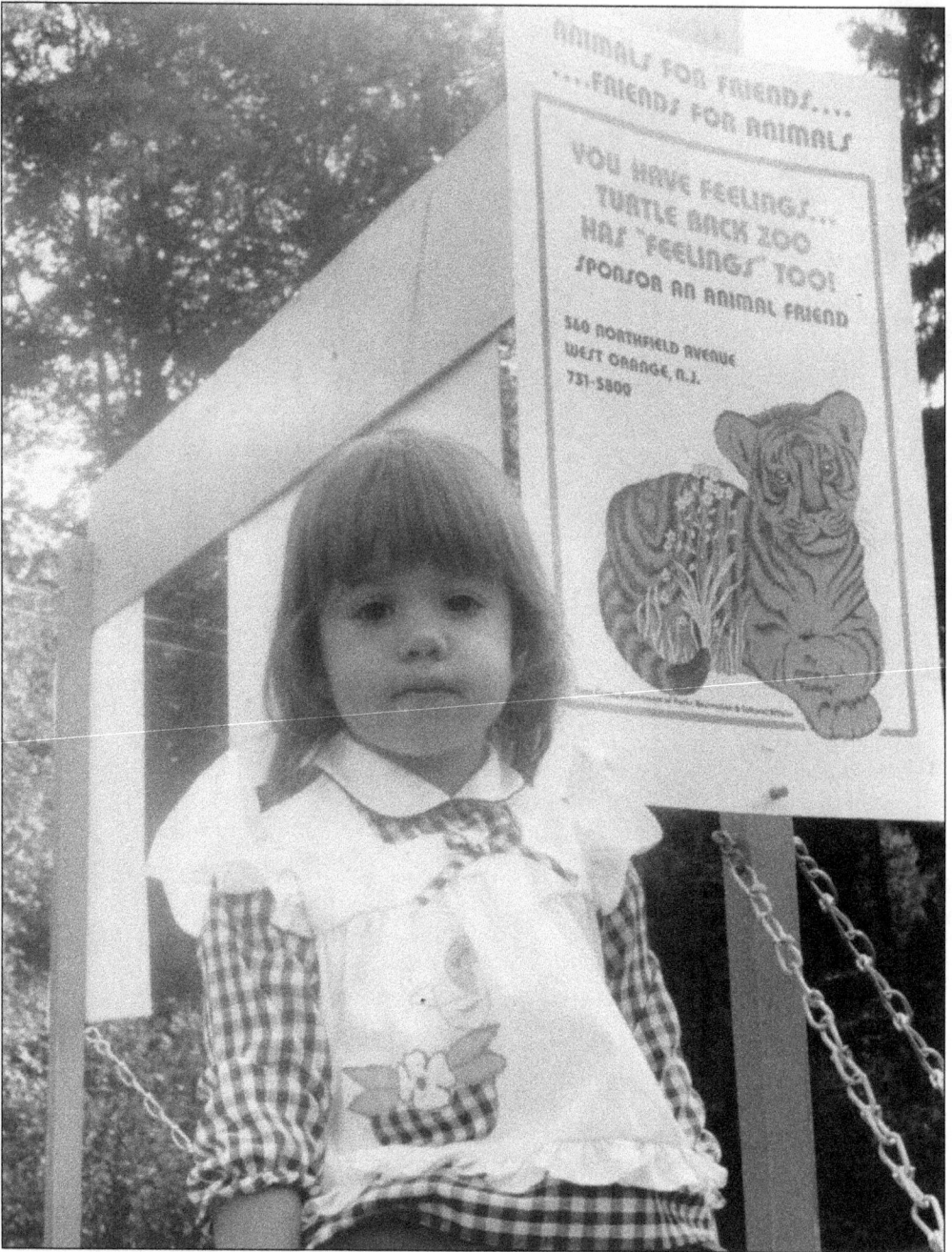

In 1987, the zoo hosted the first annual Adopt-an-Animal Party and Open House. This was the start of the Adopt-an-Animal program, which the zoo still has today. The highly successful program was begun and is still administered under the sponsorship of the Zoological Society of New Jersey, Inc. In the first two years, the program raised over $10,000. The adoption fund actually involves sponsoring, which fills a necessary and vital role at Turtle Back Zoo by helping in the feeding, care, and maintenance of the animal collection.

For several years in the 1980s, zoo educator Barbara Dyer made frequent appearances on the local *Romper Room* television show. At right, she is seen (far right) with Miss Mary Anne, a young guest, and a 200-pound Aldabra Tortoise. The tortoise was well behaved on the set but had to be watched closely off of the set. For ease of movement, the tortoise was placed on a furniture-moving dolly, but his feet could still just touch the floor. Once, while appearing on another television program, he got himself moving on the dolly and, before he could be caught, he knocked down two of the three walls of the set on which he was to appear. In the photograph below are Doo Bee (left), Miss Molly (center), and Barbara Dyer, who is holding Respect, a striped skunk from the Education Center.

Once a year, *Romper Room* would make a live stage appearance at the zoo. The event attracted thousands of fans of the popular television show to see Miss Molly and Doo Bee (above). Miss Molly became a fan of the zoo herself, going as far as donating her yellow-headed Amazon parrot, Butch, to the zoo in 1988. In 1987, Captain Kangaroo and his crew, which included Dennis and Mr. Moose, spent an entire day filming at the zoo. The Captain read stories in the midst of the goose pond and in front of the train station, and he did segments featuring many of the animals, including the kestrel, which sat on Mr. Moose's head, the screech owls, a ferret, and a fennec fox. Segments aired during November on Channel 13 at 8:00 a.m. (Courtesy of Vince Sharp.)

The Year of the Teddy Bear was declared for 1985. The Turtle Back Zoo partnered with the Good Bears of the World. Visitors were encouraged to collect new stuffed bears and drop them off at the zoo for donation to sick and abused children. Special events were held throughout the year, like the Teddy Bear Picnic (pictured here). Paddington Bear even joined the celebration!

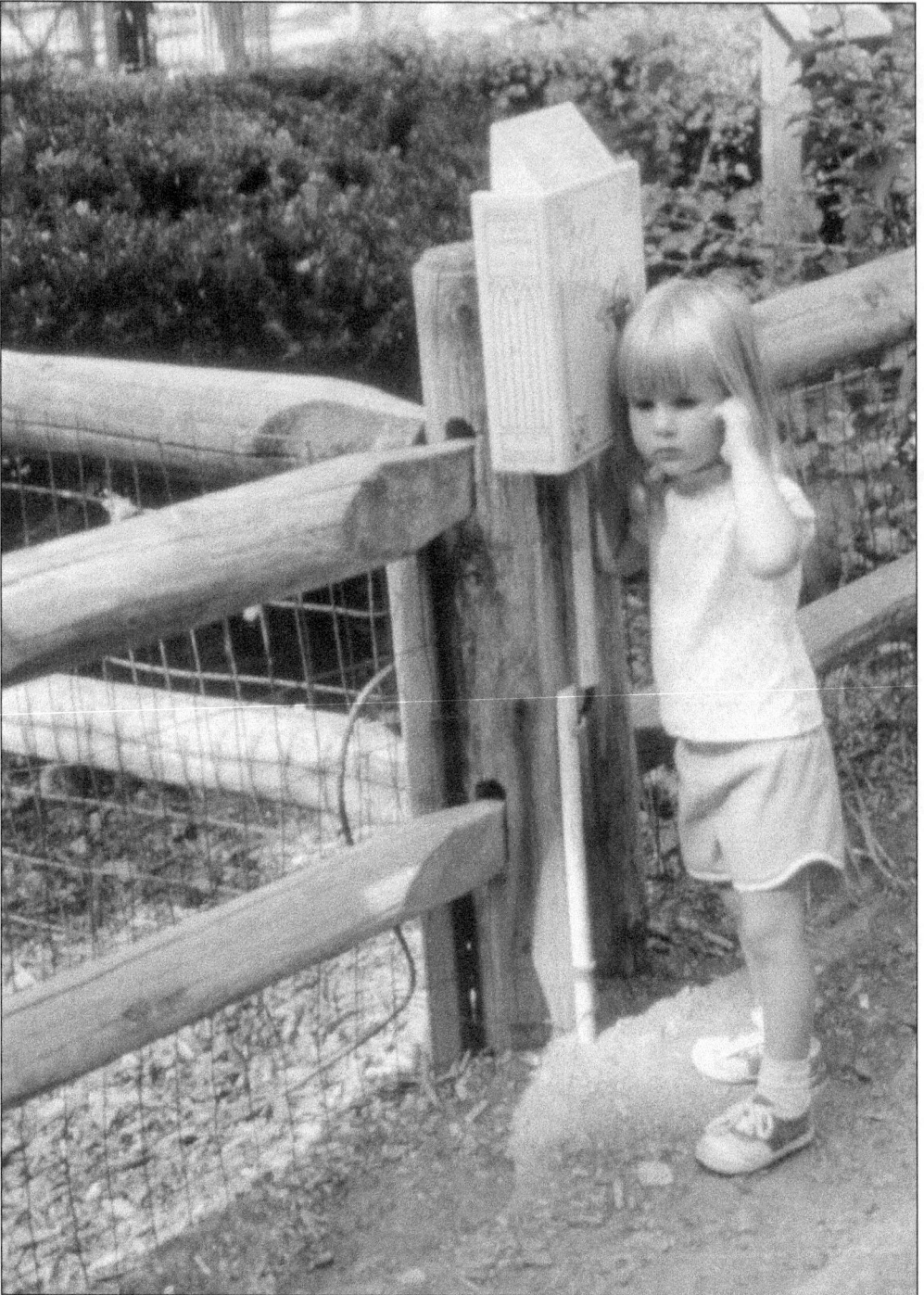

Although the Turtle Back Zoo never exhibited elephants, several million visitors associate the zoo with these creatures. Elephant-shaped keys activated the Storybook Boxes located throughout the zoo. Shown here is a young visitor listening to a tape recording of animal facts. She may be learning about the wingspan of bald eagles, the geographic range of leopards, or perhaps the adaptations of penguins.

The Storybook Boxes involved mechanical tape recorders playing a repeating one-minute message. They were very popular with visitors but a constant maintenance problem. Repeated use and year-round temperature extremes resulted in several machines out of order almost every day. Eventually, the machines' lack of dependability and cost to maintain warranted their removal.

After a few years, however, the Storybook Boxes reappeared. They had the same look but were outfitted with modern technology: digital recordings. The iconic elephant key was replaced with a plastic key card. Each year, the card's animal shape was changed to highlight a new species. These new keys, along with the old elephant keys, are considered collectibles.

Pony rides have been part of the zoo experience for young visitors for years. As the zoo expanded, the pony track was relocated many times, including by the train (now the animal hospital), by the food pavilion (now the carousel), and behind the Farm Barn. No matter where the ponies may be, the experience is the same. Rides were as much fun for parents to watch as for kids to enjoy.

The Contact Area was a place for visitors to pet and feed farm animals. One had to be careful, though, as goats did not always know the difference between the animal food the zoo sold, loose clothing, purses, shoes, or a person's lunch. One staff member was unfortunate enough to get their paycheck eaten out of their back pocket! In 1988, the Contact Area's signature turnstile gates (pictured here) were replaced by a new gate system as new fencing went up due to Wolf Woods construction.

Thursday morning, March 17, 1988, was the official ground-breaking of Wolf Woods. Part of phase one of the master plan for the zoo's New Jersey Wild theme, Wolf Woods was built over the denuded sika deer pen. A large sign declared this to be a "State of New Jersey Green Acres Project, County of Essex Wolf Exhibit." Green Acres has funded many of the zoo's improvement programs.

Once or twice a year, the zoo tries to arrange a special demonstration, where keepers have a hands-on interaction with the wolves while docents outside the exhibit interpret for the public. Keepers, taking advantage of the wolves' social nature, enter their pen to make close physical observations in order to detect any health or behavioral issues and to administer care as needed. (Courtesy of Gina Zullo.)

There were two male and two female timber wolves when Wolf Woods opened. The first "Wolf Birthday" was held in April 1991. Since then, this special event has been the unofficial kickoff of the zoo's spring season. The full day of activities includes story time, a wolf-howling contest, a clown making balloon animals, wolf videos, the Lonewolf country and western band, and a birthday-cake-cutting ceremony.

The nilgai is the largest antelope species found in Asia. They are sometimes called "blue bulls" because of the male's distinctive coloration. One winter day, staff members at the zoo were cleaning the nilgai enclosure. The male walked up behind a zookeeper, hooked his horns under her winter coat, and lifted her off the ground. A coworker saw what was happening, walked over, and rubbed the nilgai on the side until he lowered his head and put the keeper down.

Over the years, the Turtle Back Zoo has had a large and diverse collection of hoofstock. The Himalyan tahr is a goat-antelope species from the mountainous regions of India, Nepal, and Tibet. They have thick coats, as seen on this male, making them well adapted to New Jersey winters. Tahrs are a harem species; the male was housed with a number of females in a pen on the side of the mountain.

The mouflon is a species of wild sheep from mountainous areas of the Middle East. Also a harem species, they were a staple at the Turtle Back Zoo for years. Many spring lambs delighted visitors by playing in their paddock. The mouflon are believed to be the basis for many of the domestic sheep breeds existing today.

Visitors always enjoy viewing the zoo's llamas and guanacos. Over the years, many babies have been born and raised by their moms, but occasionally an animal keeper needs to provide supplemental care. Shown here is animal keeper Sue Ackerman bottle-feeding. She later went on to get her veterinarian degree. Many employees of Turtle Back went on to become veterinarians.

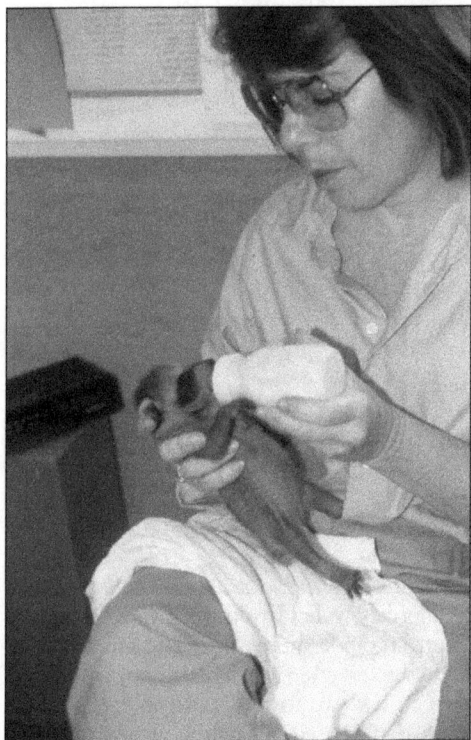

In the spring, nature's ritual of renewal produces young of many species. Different circumstances result in wild babies being separated from their mothers. When they are found, a zoo is thought of as the best place to care for them. Today, there are state-certified rehabilitators, but sometimes an animal keeper is asked to provide temporary care. Shown here is animal keeper and educator Judith Hart bottle-feeding a special formula to a baby raccoon. Many years later, Hart's zoo experience led to a generous donation to expand and remodel the zoo's administrative and educational office space.

97

Over the years, standards have changed, and zoos' operating practices have changed with them. Barriers that had once been acceptable for both the visitor and the animal were replaced with new ones that do not allow the contact visitors once enjoyed. Animal diets are more closely monitored, and public feeding is more controlled. The result is increased safety for both the animals and the visitors.

One of the zoo's most popular exhibits was the spider monkey walk. Two towers were connected by a thick rope. On each of the towers was a small hut to provide shelter from the sun and rain. A belt went around the monkey's waist and was attached to a large ring. This ring was slid over the rope so the monkey could go back and forth between the two towers. Both spider monkeys and woolly monkeys were displayed in this exhibit and then housed off-exhibit at night.

In May 1987, zoo employee Allen Foust's Australian snake-necked turtle won Best in Show at the 13th annual New York Turtle and Tortoise Society (above). The following year, Foust successfully bred rare species of turtles at Turtle Back. Foust and Turtle Back have been the proud recipients of several top awards for the species he has reproduced in the Tortoisry (below). The 12th International Symposium on Captive Propagation and Husbandry was held for three days in June 1988 in Newark, New Jersey. Many people visited the superior turtle collection at the zoo during the three days of the seminar. Walter Allen, a Californian active in turtle conservation, was so impressed that he made a donation of $1,100 to be used for a turtle project of Foust's choice.

The bald eagle exhibit was conceived, funded, and built by the zoo staff. Funding for a new exhibit was not available, but the administration gave the go-ahead if the staff could secure the funds and get volunteers to build it. Fundraising began by asking the local veterans' chapter of the 101st Airborne Division, "the Screaming Eagles," to become involved. Public Service Electric and Gas (PSE&G) volunteered to erect the telephone poles that provided the main supports for the exhibit and to put up the heavy netting used to cover the exhibit. For providing the majority of the funding, the 101st Airborne Division was given naming rights for the bald eagle. They chose the name Screaming. (Courtesy of Vince Sharp.)

Four

THE 1990S AND 2000S
MOVING FORWARD

In the early 1990s, Essex County began making funding cuts at the zoo to help reduce a budget deficit. A drop in education staff reduced the number of education programs at the zoo as well as outreach programs to schools and day-care centers. Work was halted on the new Animal Hospital and Isolation Center, as funds that had previously been allocated were no longer available. The process to receive accreditation from the Association of Zoos and Aquariums (AZA) had to be put on hold as staff and supporters readjusted their focus from expansion to just keeping the doors open.

The impending zoo closure rallied the local community to speak up. Letters from children and their parents flooded county officials' offices. Students sold T-shirts to raise money for the zoo. In March 1996, a children's rally in the zoo parking lot, organized by the Zoological Society of New Jersey, involved about 300 school-age children. Their message: the zoo was a unique part of the community and should not be forgotten. There were talks of public-private partnerships, but in the end the zoo remained a county facility under the parks department. With renewed zeal, renovation and new development planning was underway.

By 2000, the zoo completed a new master plan, with accreditation from AZA as a major focus. Outdated, 1960s-style caging began to be replaced with larger, naturalistic habitats for the animals. At the end of the year, the otter and cat exhibits were opened, along with a new entrance plaza. In 2005, the on-grounds Essex County Animal Hospital was built. The original administration buildings and education center were demolished, and a new picnic pavilion and animal-themed playground were added in 2006, but the highlight was the long-awaited accreditation by the AZA. The growth continued, and the zoo added Wild New Jersey in 2007, and Australian Exhibit in 2008, gibbons in 2009, an aquarium in 2010, and Big Cat Country in 2011.

The Turtle Back Zoo celebrated its 50th anniversary in 2013. An anniversary logo, created to showcase the celebratory year, was prominently displayed on staff shirts, banners, and souvenirs. The zoo also created a time capsule containing historical items to be opened on its 100th anniversary.

When the zoo remodeled the front entrance, there was a desire to create an air of excitement. After walking through the iconic turrets, visitors are met by a life-sized bronze Komodo dragon sculpture by Tom Tischler. This statue is located in front of a small pool and waterfall surrounded by thick plantings. The combination of a large animal sculpture and natural plantings subtly lets visitors know what to expect during their visit.

For select weekends during the summer, the zoo brought in special guest animals. One of the most popular was Teddy the giraffe. Teddy made several visits to the zoo. A temporary enclosure was made by fencing off a section between the education and administration buildings. A coin-operated feed dispenser gave visitors the opportunity to give Teddy treats. Giraffes, as well as elephants and camels, came to the zoo for a day with the help of R.W. Commerford, a Connecticut-based farm that provides animals for various events.

In 1998, the zoo had two events with elephant rides. The second one, in September, featured Asian elephants Minnie and Beulah. It was estimated that over 1,000 people took the unique journey around the grounds on Saturday alone. It is interesting to note that R.W. Commerford was the farm where the zoo rented its petting zoo and pony ride animals for visitors to enjoy during the summer months before the current Farm Barn at the top of the zoo was built.

Animal keepers are encouraged to suggest and implement exhibit habitat enhancement and animal enrichment opportunities; sometimes, a whole new exhibit is conceived and constructed by keepers. The trout tank is a good example of this. Keeper Frank Fink was an avid trout fisherman and mason. With donated cinder block and a leftover glass panel from the South Mountain arena, an exhibit space for rainbow and brook trout was built. The exhibit was open-air, but the public viewing area was enclosed to aid visibility.

Chester, an Arctic fox, was obtained from the Terry Lou Zoo. Approximately one year old when obtained, Chester was born with an incurable but treatable eye infection. A prominent display animal during the winter months, Chester was moved to a cooler, shady area when spring arrived. These types of seasonal moves happen throughout the zoo.

Otters have been part of the zoo since the 1970s. Over the years, renovations have taken place to their exhibit space. The zoo has taken on a lead role in the conservation of otters, including hosting the first otter captive-breeding symposium. Some of the otter pups born at the zoo were used in the zoo education programs.

Deborah Guarino came to the Turtle Back Zoo to do a reading and signing of her book, *Is Your Mama a Llama?*, which was published in 1997. It was known around the zoo that Guarino came to Turtle Back to observe the llamas for illustration inspiration.

For a number of years, Turtle Back Zoo was invited to the Cathedral of Saint John the Divine in New York City for the Blessing of the Animals on the first Sunday in October. At the end of an environmentally themed Mass, up to 100 animals were blessed at the altar. Animals from all over the world, from different habitats and of different sizes, were in attendance. Among the creatures being blessed were an elephant, a mouse, a bald eagle, a chicken, lizards, frogs, fish, and insects. The zoo would usually bring a hedgehog, African penguin, tawny frogmouth, boa constrictor, leopard tortoise, tarantula, and Madagascar hissing roaches. Those attending the service could bring their household pets. One might expect a chaotic scene, but calm silence was the general mood. Animal keepers remember the service as "a lifetime experience" that is often reflected upon. Shown in the photograph above are, from left to right, Tina Silvestro holding a tawny frogmouth, Naomi Specht holding an American kestrel, Kelly Lauer holding an African penguin, Bonnie Sippie holding a leopard tortoise, and Vince Sharp holding a boa constrictor.

On November 14, 1998, a striking sculpture was unveiled at Turtle Back Zoo. Created by Kristine Smock, a native of Essex Fells, it is a cultural addition to the grounds. The welded metal sculpture, located in the grassy area behind the Joe the Crow exhibit, depicts a male deer with antlers. Integrated into the sculpture is an assortment of wild animals and the message, "Walking in Nature Wilderness to our Limits Transformed." Smock, at one time a Zooette, spent many happy hours at Turtle Back. Her uncle, William Bartholomew of Essex Fells, commissioned and donated this sculpture titled, *We Are One*.

This is a good example of staff recycling an exhibit space. Originally the tapir pool at the south end of the Red Barn, this exhibit was reworked to showcase reptiles. Many species of freshwater and land turtles, as well as a caiman, cycled through this exhibit. The naturalistic habitat made the inhabitants sometimes tricky to locate, and visitors would have to spend time trying to count as many turtles as they could find.

Lady Lurch was donated to the zoo when her owners could no longer safely care for the seven-foot Burmese python. Within a few years, she rapidly grew to be a 200-pound, 17-foot specimen that could eat a rabbit every other week. This is a good example of how some animals are just not suited to be pets. It took about six people to hold her. Although quite large, because of the care and handling of the zoo education staff Lady Lurch was able to be safely utilized during special occasions. Holding the snake are, from left to right, zoo supervisor Gina Zullo, docent Kathy Dowling, educator Vince Sharp, zookeeper Alan Faust, and docent Naomi Specht.

The ABC House (above) has held many different animals throughout the years, like two fennec foxes (at left). The ABC House was initially used to hold live animals for education programming. It was not an exhibit space at the time. The space was turned into an aviary when the new Education Center was built. The installation of a large window allowed the exhibit space to house, when needed, mammals like the fennec fox or reptiles like the Burmese python.

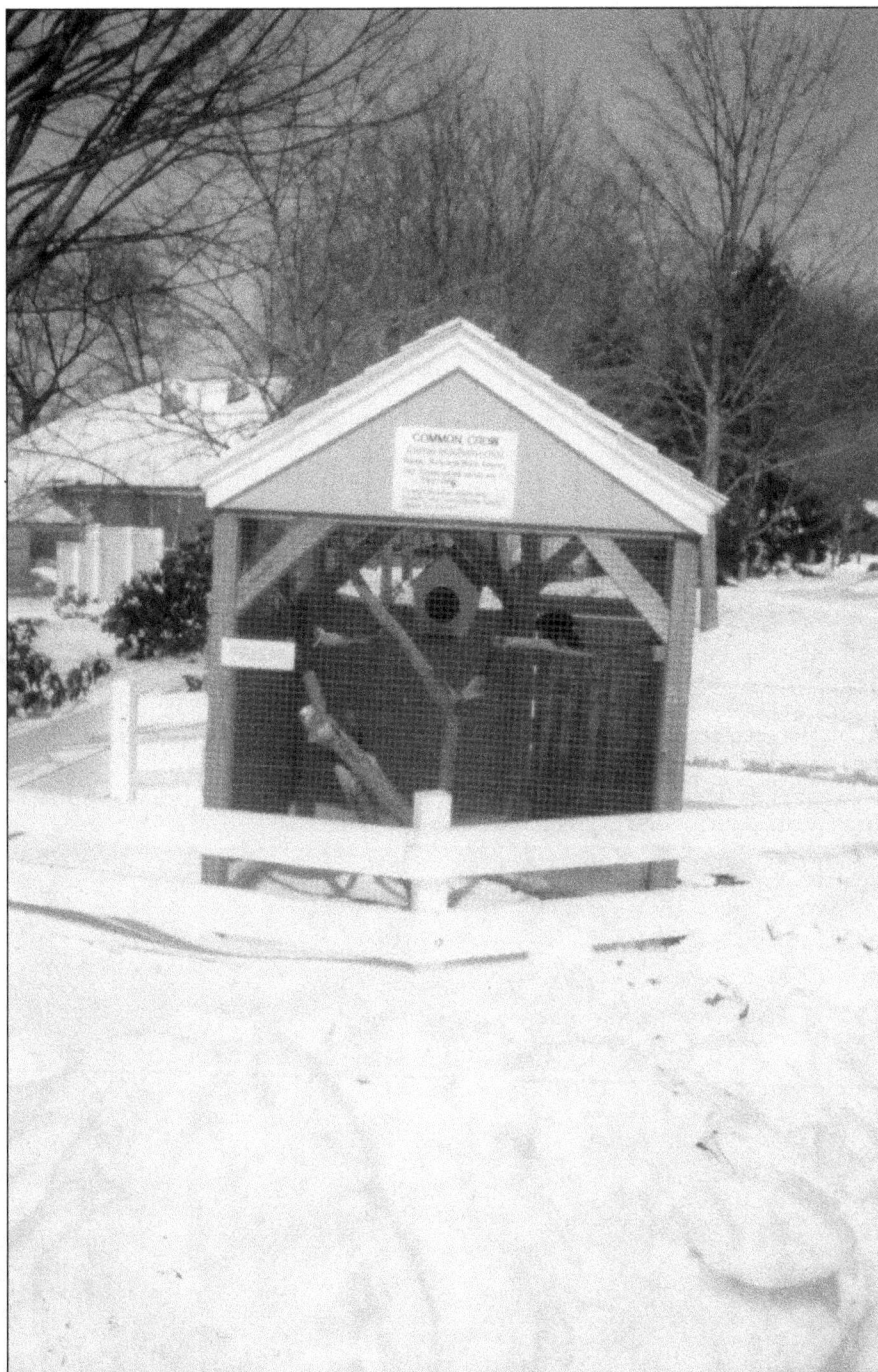

Located close to the zoo entrance, Joe the Crow was, for many visitors, the first animal they encountered. Joe took on the role of zoo greeter. Unpaid—but well fed—he would greet guests with "Hello, I'm a crow." In addition to speaking, Joe would frequently confuse guests by crowing like a rooster. Joe arrived at the zoo as an injured bird and was rehabilitated, but he was unable to be released. This is the case with many of the birds at the zoo. Joe quickly became a favorite, entertaining visitors for over 25 years.

In 2005, the zoo opened Bears in Your Backyard, a black bear exhibit designed to illustrate the relationship between bears and people in New Jersey. The public viewing space is designed to look like a house, with the bears in the "backyard." A refrigerator in the kitchen displays favorite bear foods, and a television plays a feature on living with bears produced by the New Jersey Department of Environmental Protection's Division of Fish and Wildlife.

In 2005, the zoo opened the $1.8 million Animal Hospital to care for the animals and serve as a quarantine facility for a growing collection. The veterinary suite includes treatment, surgery, x-ray, and necropsy rooms. The quarantine side has holding rooms for large and small mammals and two rooms for reptiles and birds. A set of outside stalls holds hoofstock.

In preparation for AZA accreditation and as a result of the rapid growth of the zoo, the master plan was rewritten in 2006. The zoo was moving from being a random collection of animal enclosures to one organized around geographic regions and habitats. This allowed the zoo to more easily convey educational and conservation messages to the visitors. One of the first areas to begin construction under the new plan was Amazing Asia. With this, the zoo was able to accommodate two new Species Survival Plan (SSP) species, Amur leopards and red pandas.

When the Big Cat exhibit opened in the North American section in 2011, the zoo's resident cougars moved to the new exhibit. Their former space was then converted for snow leopards, and the transition of Amazing Asia was complete. The acquisition of snow leopards continued the zoo's commitment to conservation by working with more SSP species. In 2012, the zoo received a breeding recommendation for snow leopards, and the institution's first potential breeding pair was formed. Previously, snow leopards had been housed in the Star of the Zoo cage (below).

The zoo added a carousel in 2008 as a value-added attraction for the visitor. Custom designed for the Turtle Back Zoo, it features replicas of more than 30 endangered species (and a dragon) instead of the typical carousel horses. The $3,637,000 project includes a small building for food concessions, restrooms, and an outdoor patio. This area can be used as rental space for private parties. Energy conservation features include exterior LED lighting and a radiant floor heating system.

The Tam-Ring Gibbon Reserve is the cornerstone of the Amazing Asia area. The 30-foot-tall exhibit recreates an Asian temple ruin as an archeological site. Scaffolding and cargo boxes add visual appeal for the visitors and climbing structures for the gibbons. Adjacent exhibits include white-naped cranes and muntjacs. A small meditation garden provides a quiet retreat for the visitor. A design concept in the current master plan was to include an auditory component to each section. The gibbons often sing duets in the morning to announce their territory, and this was the auditory component for the Asian section.

115

In 2008, the Australian Walkabout area was opened. The exhibit includes a free-flight aviary. Shown at the ribbon-cutting ceremony (above) are county executive Joseph DiVincenzo (center, with scissors), officials from the County Parks and Public Works Departments, architects, and construction-company representatives. The Zoological Society of New Jersey provided a grant to cover the cost of the exhibit's construction. The $1.17 million renovation of the Australian section was paid for by state Green Acres money and funds from the Essex County capital budget.

The 40-foot-by-80-foot walk-through aviary features 500 free-flight parakeets. Visitors are able to purchase a feed stick and offer it to the birds as they walk through. Two separate enclosures within this larger structure house kookaburras, tawny frogmouths, and lories. This interactive aviary helps to promote the zoo's mission of strengthening the bond between people and animals.

Big Cat Country opened in 2011. This exhibit moved the cougars out of the Asian section and into the North American section. It also allowed the zoo to add jaguars to the animal collection. The exhibit was designed to look like an abandoned southwest US mine, helping to show the connection between people and animal habitats. The recirculating pool in the jaguar exhibit was designed to operate at a more shallow depth in the event that the zoo receives a breeding recommendation and produces cubs.

In 2012, the Turtle Back Zoo exhibited its first Komodo dragon. Shu was born at the Sedgwick County Zoo in Wichita, Kansas, in 2008. Interestingly, he was a parthenogenetic birth resulting from a form of asexual reproduction. Approximately 70 species of vertebrates are able to reproduce in this fashion. It is believed that this reproductive strategy is useful for species that may colonize an island but not have any potential mates.

To add a new dimension to the visitor experience, the zoo opened a walk-through butterfly exhibit in 2012. Visitors enter a nylon-mesh tunnel made in the form of a caterpillar. Inside are over 500 butterflies and a large variety of nectar plants. There are two smaller enclosures displaying different life stages: the first has caterpillars on host plants, and the second has a rack for displaying chrysalises as they prepare to emerge.

To celebrate its 50th anniversary, the zoo undertook its most ambitious project to date, opening Sea Lion Sound. The 100,000-gallon outdoor sea lion pool is almost eight times larger than the pool that held sea lions in the 1970s. The new system contains saltwater, which is healthier for the animals. Inside the building is a 3,000-gallon touch tank with stingrays and sharks.

As zoos have advanced, more emphasis has been placed on the mental health and well-being of the animals. Training and enrichment have grown in importance as animal management tools. A local group of home-school students was studying predators and prey. They created a papier-mâché capybara for the zoo's cougar (seen here). Zookeepers put a portion of the cat's diet inside, and the students were able to observe the cat attacking its food.

Zookeepers give talks to the public on a daily basis. These educational programs are an important means of connecting the visitors with the animals. Topics vary depending on the exhibit and species, but they usually include conservation and natural history. The most popular talks include a training session in which the keepers demonstrate positive-reinforcement techniques used to manage the animal collection.

Another important message that zoos deliver is that wild animals do not make good pets. Zookeepers are able to work in close proximity to wild animals by following established safety procedures and not treating the animals like pets. During public feeding demonstrations, zookeepers use long tongs and stand behind a safety barrier.

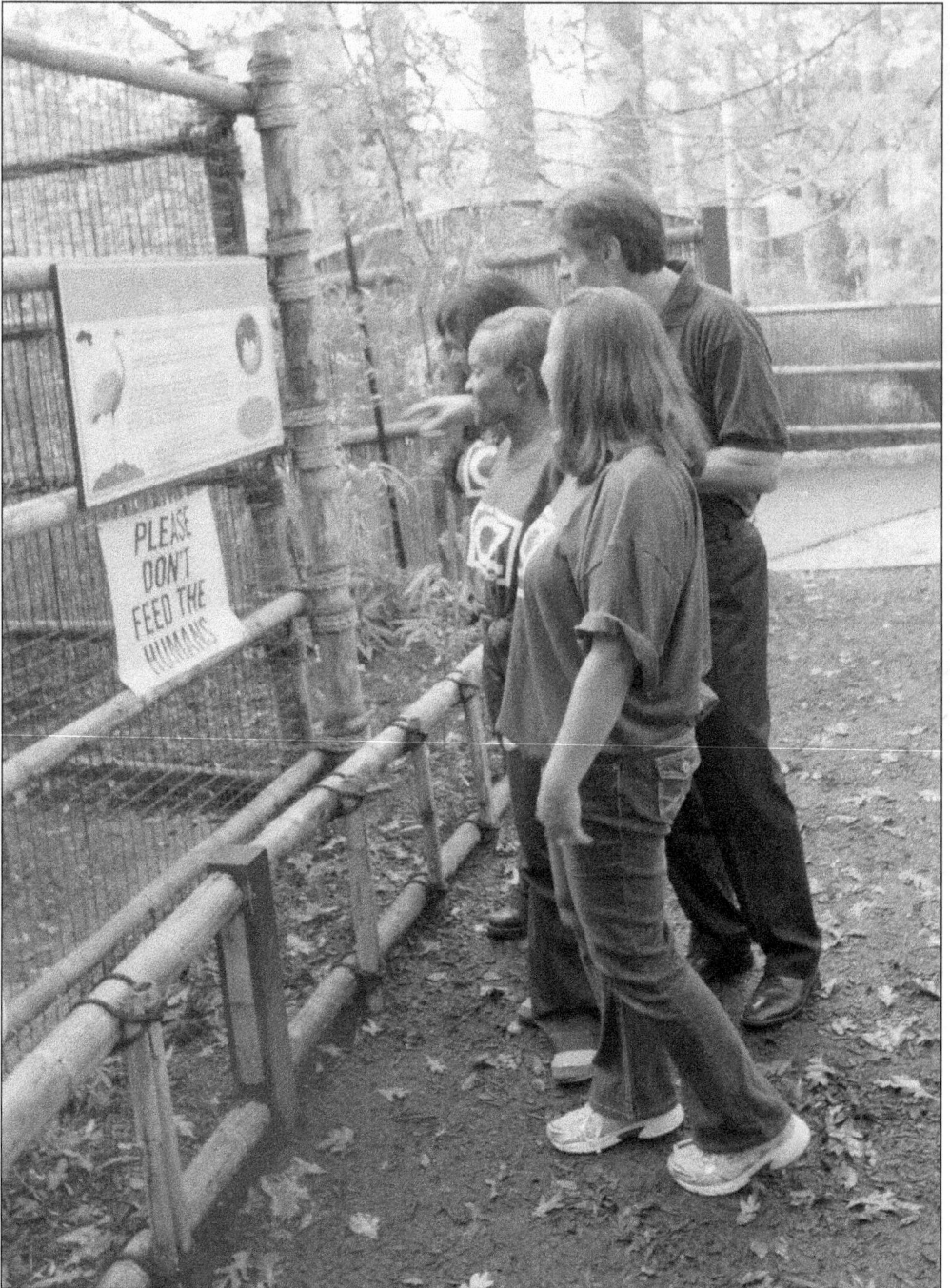

Being close to New York City, the Turtle Back Zoo is often tapped to assist with various television productions. In October 2011, *The Dr. Oz Show* used the zoo as the site for an episode on prehistoric diets. Three volunteers were "locked" in a cage at the zoo and fed a diet of fruits and vegetables to see if this primitive diet would lower their blood pressure, cholesterol, and weight.

Sometimes, the zoo staff just wants to have fun. In 2012, when the New York Giants played the New England Patriots in Super Bowl XLVI, keepers showed support for the home team as well as creativity by hosting an animal-themed pep rally. Animal exhibits were decorated with red and blue banners, encouraging the Giants. The banners were made of pre-approved, animal-safe enrichment materials.

In 2012, the zoo celebrated the Chinese Year of the Dragon by opening a Komodo dragon exhibit. Festivities were held throughout the year to explore dragons in different cultures. One weekend, a traveling group of players from the Medieval Times Castle in Lyndhurst, New Jersey, came to the zoo. The king, princess, and members of the royal court performed for visitors.

When the Blue Man Group was looking for a location to film a segment for their live show in New York City, they came to the Turtle Back Zoo and enlisted the help of zoo staff, zoo campers, docents, and visitors. Participants held up letters to form the lyrics for The Beatles song "The Word." The resulting film was shown as a backdrop for the stage show. (Courtesy of Mike Kolatac.)

On October 29, 2012, Superstorm Sandy struck New Jersey. This storm was the second-most costly in US history. At the Turtle Back Zoo, over 80 trees, mostly Norway spruce, were uprooted at each end of the complex. The Treetop Adventures aerial ropes course, which had opened the previous year, was totally destroyed. Almost 40 trees around the zoo train were blown down, causing damage to the track and the train barn.

As part of the zoo's 50th anniversary celebration, television personality and Columbus Zoo director emeritus Jack Hanna toured the zoo and then gave a public presentation in nearby Cody Arena. During his visit, Hanna described the Turtle Back Zoo as "one of the finest zoos in the country." Shown here are county executive Joseph DiVincenzo (left), Hanna (center), and zoo director Dr. Jeremy Goodman.

The concept of habitat—"adequate unpolluted food and water, safe shelter options, and enough space to sustain a species population"—is a common thread in all zoo education programming. Zoo educators Stephanie Bradley (left) and Caitlin Sharp hold planet Earth, the habitat of the human species. Creating lasting connections between humans, other species, and our shared habitat is a goal when addressing any visitor. It is a hope that these connections will then lead to environmentally conscious behaviors to help sustain our world for the generations to come—human and animal alike. (Courtesy of Vince Sharp.)

Visit us at
arcadiapublishing.com

9 781531 672393